THE TRIAL OF
MY FAITH

BY PATRICK J. DIGGS, PASTOR

Foreword by Mary A. Diggs

Copyright © 2013 Patrick J. Diggs and BLI Publishing

ISBN: 0615904262
ISBN-13: 978-0615904269

Published by:

BLI Publishing

DeSoto, TX 75115

info@TheBLIGroupLLC.com
www.TheBLIGroupLLC.com
Local: (469) 557-1254

Printed in the United States of America via CreateSpace.com

Published in October 2013

TABLE OF CONTENT

DEDICATION

I dedicate this book to everyone who has ever had to overcome the negative emotions from being called and chosen by God. This book will help you understand that your calling has a greater purpose but you have to keep going because your reward from God will always be greater than your trials.

FOREWORD

Often when we go through trials, we think God is punishing us. It's not until the trial is over, that we realize He was exonerating us and elevating us. That's the essence of *The Trial of My Faith*. It's an in depth look, at one of the most trying times in my husband's life and ministry. Because Satan attacked his faith, the faith of our entire family was placed on trial. Every aspect of our life was put to the test. The good news is, we were found GUILTY… guilty of trusting in God!

I commend my husband and pastor for being transparent and sharing the intimate details of his faith attack. The man I know and love doesn't wear his feelings on his sleeve, so it was not an easy task for him to share them with all of you. As difficult as this book was for him to write, he deemed it necessary. Why? Because people need to understand that spiritual attacks are real. When they come, we can't revert back to our carnal methods of counter attack. We have to use spiritual weapons to win spiritual battles. In reading *The Trial of My Faith*, you'll identify with Pastor Diggs' humanity and will ultimately be drawn to his spirituality.

If you're struggling through a trying period in your life, this is the book for you. It will not only encourage you, but it will also equip you with the tools needed to survive and thrive in the midst of your trial. Although this book captures one of the toughest periods in our lives and ministry, I'm grateful that God allowed the trial. Without it, we wouldn't have the marriage or the ministry that we have today!

It is my hope that as a result of reading *The Trial of My Faith* that you too will be found GUILTY... guilty of trusting in God!

Love and Blessings,
Mary A. Diggs

"Consider it all joy, my brethren, when you encounter various trials, knowing that the testing of your faith produces endurance. And let endurance have its perfect result, so that you may be perfect and complete, lacking nothing." James 1:2-4 (NASB)

PREFACE

I never imagined that God would use me for something that I would consider to be the most painful experience of my life. I knew that I would be used to change the lives of those He called me to lead but I didn't think that I would be used to experience the pain that I experienced for three years of my life. What God did for me during the building process of New Fellowship Church of Fort Worth was bigger than I could have ever experienced. I got to see lives changes, hopes and dream restored, and the true salvation of God in the restoration of our ministry and in me.

I was a man who devoted his life to being the underdog. There was no greater joy than to prove to anyone that I could do something they said that I couldn't. I was hardening my heart and God knew that in order to use me the way He needed to use me I would have to be completely broken. I was challenged because when the attacks started I only saw the pain that I was being caused by the members of the church. Therefore, I made it a point to fight them with my integrity and character, things they didn't care about. Eventually, I had to surrender it all to God and that's when He began to show me that I was causing the delay because I was not fighting them fully in the spirit of the Lord.

We have to get like that… stop fighting in the natural and see that there are demonic forces out there that do nothing more than try to keep you fighting in the natural. When God calls you, let Him truly use you. Give it all to Him even those things you think you can handle without God.

This book is a book that will help you move past your pains without the hurt and break free of some of the strong holds you may have placed on your life. I am here to tell you that it is okay to be frustrated, angry, and bitter from the things you go through when you allow God to use you. What's not okay is giving up and agreeing to stay put in those emotions and feelings. Let it go so God can show you and others in your life who He is and why you were called.

Enjoy reading.

INTRODUCTION

I can't believe that He set me up. After all I've given up for Him and He set me up like this? When I was going through my three year season of trials and tribulation from building our new church, I couldn't help but to feel as if the God that called me and the God that I was calling on had set me up.

If you have ever felt like you've been set up to be used (regardless if it's by God or someone else), then grab a notebook and pen because there will be a lot of important lessons that you will need to learn. My hope is that you will learn that when you are called by God to lead people that persecution will come and it will come even when you are innocent of all accusations that are brought against you. Hopefully you will learn that the testing and trying of your faith will increase your trust in God. You will learn that nothing hurts more than watching the people that said they would be there for you lead the charges of defamation.

Yes, the lessons of God are profound when you open your mouth to utter the words, "Lord, use me." I uttered those words. Though I meant every utterance, I didn't realize what it would take to be on trial every day for three years of my life. I never thought that I could experience so much mental anguish while trying to determine why God was allowing me to be persecuted on the same platform He called me preach on. I felt alone and honestly there were days where I wanted God Himself to end my life so I wouldn't have to bear a cross that I thought I never deserved. But in hindsight, I deserved all of it because my persecution became my testimony. It allowed me to minister from a different perspective. God stretched me past my own limitations and understandings. I admit I still get frustrated when I think about some of the trials I endured for those three years but I also know that it was for His glory and with that I can't complain.

Imagine being set up by God. That's right, being setup but the one that called you to be in a particular position. That's like your teacher calling you to be the teacher's aide for the day because she knows you are a good student but then shaming you knowing you did nothing wrong. Imagine calling out to God every day, every hour, every minute, or even every second and not hearing Him because to you He has shut you out and you don't know why. We have all been there where we felt completely abandoned by God after He called us into a position or even into place. We just said, "Lord, I will go" and it seemed He went.

I remember my days as an athlete. I was dedicated and committed to being the best. I had the mentality that everything I did, everything that I wanted to become was in my control and within my grasp. All I had to do was reach out and take what I felt was mine. I would train longer and harder than any of my teammates. I got up before everyone else, regardless of what I did the night before and I was the last one to leave because I believed in my heart that I had something to prove. I believed that I was better than everyone else who was bigger than me, smarter than me, and taller than me.

In my youth, I was always determined to fight against people and things because I thought I was in control but in all honesty, those things were in control of me. My fight, my drive to be better had a strong hold on me. My determination to be more than the ordinary would be what God used to set me up in front of those He called me to lead. It was irony at its finest because while I making myself a fighter, God was making me into a warrior. He had to break the spirit of fight that I had and He replaced it with the heart of a servant, the convictions of a leader and the skilled mindset of a warrior.

Just know that when you step up to be used by God, when you say, "Lord, here I am… use me," then you essentially tell God that you are willing to die to yourself and all of your own personal beliefs and convictions. You tell God that you are ready to be positioned for what He wants you to accomplish. So I would strongly caution you to not speak those words unless you are absolutely willing to be used by God, even when it hurts.

Job 13:6 became my personal testimony during the longest trial of my life. In this setting, God was the judge, even though I was standing before Him worshipping and praising Him every day. He had me on public display to show that I am not a fighter but His warrior. The people He called me to lead were the jury. Some even volunteered to be the prosecution, right along with the devil himself. But oh, my Lord I am glad that Jesus was my defense attorney and every day He briefed me to stand my ground, to not give up, that the battles and trials that I was about to face were not all about me but those that needed to be freed from their own personal bondage.

Can you imagine being on trial after you have been called? I asked this question so many times during my life. I couldn't imagine why I gave my life to a God that would make me out to be the bad guy. But didn't He change the life of Noah, a drunk? Didn't He change the life of Paul? Didn't He give Job to the devil? I can go on and on about who God used and they would probably feel how I felt, 'Lord why did you bring me out to set me up?'

The call of a pastor is one that I have taken seriously since I realized that God was going to use me in a major way. I never knew how but I was always open to the thought of being used by God. Just think about God using you to advance His kingdom. For me it still sends chills up my spine that the Lord believes that I have what it takes to lead His precious flock. I knew there would be persecution, deception, and lies but I never imagined how close to home those things would come. How I would lose countless hours of my life, worrying, crying, cussing, and doubting that I was even called. Don't be alarmed at the fact that I added cussing because I am not a preacher that seeks the next opportunity to show people I can talk God, I live God, and I deal with a flock that deals with life while searching for the God that I so boldly bragged about. I deal in the real world but I am not defined by it.

In 2006, I was called to be a pastor. I remember feeling that there would come a time during my calling that I would be expected to stand on the word of God alone. Now I knew that I always had to stand on the word of God alone, but during this process I realized that the conviction of me standing bold on God's word would mean that even if I looked guilty I couldn't walk away. I knew that I would have to face rejection and tense times would be a normal occurrence in my life. Especially from people who failed to seek God's heart for themselves. These were the people who perfected the traditional roles of church attendees. The ones that praised and worshipped on cue, either as the preacher hooped or as the choir sang and when it all stopped so did they. The same people that stood in unity to select me were the same ones, who with no solid evidence or real knowledge of anything would persecute me to the fullest of their understanding. But limited understanding didn't include the word of God or the vision of the ministry they said they were led to.

How is that? How are people able to condemn and persecute someone that they said were called to lead them? Simple. They never trusted God's will or way and they had become fashioned with the role of a churchgoer rather than the role of a God seeker. Despite seeing the role players I did notice the God seekers and I was becoming the man that openly praised God, the man who cried out loud and testified to God's glory, and the believer in His goodness. My life experiences conditioned me for the tough times that were ahead of me. I knew that as God was opening my heart to receive His word and His power that I would be faced with an impossible situation. That my faith would be all I had to rely on and turn to. I knew and believed that one day God would answer my challenge and put me in a situation that looked impossible to be in and to do.

I was convicted that my standing bold on the impossible would make naysayers accuse me of ill intentions, deceit, and outright debauchery. I didn't realize then that God was not only the judge in all of this; He was my confidant and my Father. He was stern enough to not pull me from the fire but compassionate enough to shield me from being harmed. So I had to develop a heart for God during my trials and early morning sessions with just Him and me. My heart had to be emotionally softened to receive the pain tolerance of a leader.

HEARING FROM GOD

When you are called to be the leader that God is leading you to be then you have to allow God to emotionally soften you and to build your pain tolerance so you can lead those who you have been called to be lead. You have to be determined enough to spend time alone with God so you can hear from Him, without interruptions. You have to develop a love for hearing God speak clearly through you. So many people don't understand that if they listen carefully the clouds will talk, the wind will whisper in your ear, and silence will reveal truths. You just have to learn to discern the voice of God. It's a wonderful voice that convicts and moves every doubt, if allowed. For me, hearing God speak so clearly developed in me a tough exterior while softening my interior. In those quiet conversations, I realized that I was becoming a man after God's own heart. So when I was faced with the impossible, I knew that I couldn't reject being used and act like I never knew God was setting me up for something greater than myself.

When you have a heart for God you have a heart that is subjected to being broken by the people closest to you. You have to be willing to be trained to commit to a life of discipline and re-condition yourself to be durable. It is important that you learn to control your natural emotions and respond in the supernatural anointing of the Holy Spirit and not your natural self. I know it seems challenging because we are all in this world but you must remember that we are not of this world.

David was chosen by God to become king when he was just a shepherd boy. No one, not his brothers or his parents, thought he was qualified to be a leader. I'm sure he knew that he wasn't good enough to them but that didn't stop him from conditioning himself daily as he tended and cared for the sheep he was assigned to watch. He mastered his fear by defeating a lion and a bear that imposed danger to his flock. He controlled his emotions when he was constantly rejected by those closest to him. I had to learn to be like David, steadfast in my desires to protect my flock and controlled in my emotions that even though when those who claimed to be with me doubted, denied and persecuted me that I still had to love them enough to not hate them and to lead them to God.

Let's take a closer look at David, the boy king. When Jesse came to anoint a king, his parents and brothers rejected him but yet he was still chosen and anointed. He didn't lead then but the calling was on his life. Knowing He would he would be king, David didn't run away from the call because of the unfamiliar. Don't we often run from our calling and refuse our anointing because we don't want to fight giants? Do you think David would have willingly agreed to be anointed if he knew that in his life he would be accused, rejected and persecuted? Probably not. When Goliath and the Philistines came against the army, David, who was sent to bring food and water to his brothers, stepped up to challenge and defeat Goliath, but instead of being welcomed as a warrior his motives were questioned by his own brothers. I Samuel 17:28 says, *When Eliab, David's oldest brother, heard him speaking with the men, he burned with anger at him and asked, "Why have you come down here? And with whom did you leave those few sheep in the wilderness? I know how conceited you are and how wicked your heart is; you came down only to watch the battle." Imagine what it feels like to be challenged by those who you have come to save.*

I have learned that sometimes innocence and righteousness are complete strangers, especially when you are being persecuted by people who say they love, respect, and cherish you. The pain of being persecuted by those who sought me and said I was their preacher, is something that I will never forget. I have forgiven those individuals who sought to destroy my character, my name, and at times even tested my faith in myself as their pastor. I decided to write this book about the faith I had to endure, yes, I said endure to understand how to discover the fullness and closeness I would need to have with God.

My journey of having my faith placed on trial for three years is a true testament of my God-given purpose to learn from people who were in pain. This book will help you properly manage the pain in your life after you have been chosen but then persecuted for having faith in God that He put you where you are, whether it's currently, in the past or coming soon. Pain is inevitable when you trust and believe God with everything you are and everything you know, even when it doesn't make sense to anyone else not even you.

I remember telling myself countless times that my faith was the evidence of things hoped for. That I had to forsake the things that were temporary, which included the persecution, the hatred I experienced week in and week out, and the lies that were constantly told against me. I had to tell myself that God was using me for a purpose that was bigger than myself. But do you realize how hard it is to preach to individuals who sought you out and then reject you as their leader? These people that trusted me to lead them were the same people who started all of the charges and false witnessing against me. I will tell you it's no walk in the park to see these people and still be obedient to the will of God. It was never easy.

It was hard because I knew they made up lies against my character, they lied against my family, they just plain old lied. I think the most hurtful aspect of their false allegations is that they were never able to produce evidence to support their claims of wrong doings. I opened up the church financial records for them to review, but they never found evidence that I was stealing money. I had an open door policy, that I still have to this day, but they never used it … instead they would collectively gather in the church parking lot as a way to condemn me. They would even be so bold to be sit in the presence of God every Sunday and refuse to allow the Holy Spirit to have any control in their lives.

Those were shameful times. Not only for me but for those individuals who were on their own individual assignments from Satan to diminish the man of God. Yes, I said on assignment from Satan because I know my God is not the author of confusion. And these persecutors attempted daily in their lives and mine to deliver nothing but confusion. They were filled with so much hate that you could literally feel it when they entered into a room. The air was sucked out and a sense of dishonor and confusion ushered its way in.

I surrendered precious hours of sleep to get out in various weather temperatures, as if I was being paid to do so, to work out, and have alone time with God. It was my way of getting away from the monotony in hopes of enjoying quiet time with God - no phones ringing, no urgent meetings, not even a chirp from the early rising birds in the neighborhood. If I was going to be focused in the future, the way I'd been focused in the past, I would have to be intentional about my devotion time with my boss. This was a time of reflection for me. A time of venting where I was able to be 100% honest with God.

During my reflections I realized that I had been in church all my life and I was always able to identify people who had perfected the traditionalism of church. The people who if you crossed paths with you believed that they were genuine believers. Life experiences had been teaching me how to condition myself for the testing times ahead. I was beginning to think that one day

I would be faced with an impossible situation that my faith would be all I had to depend on if I was to get through it. I believed that I would do something that looked impossible. What I didn't know or rather what I didn't realize is that in doing the impossible, I would be sending an invitation to the enemy to investigate my motives and agenda. It was the power of accomplishing what seemed incredible and impossible that would raise questions.

So my 5:00 a.m. workouts not only helped my physical being, it soften my heart emotionally. I developed a heart for God during all those hours looking into the sky and listening to the clouds. I would learn to be soft enough to comfort and stern enough to correct because I would hear things in my near future that would kill me or create in me a balanced behavior in ministry. I knew what I was hearing was going to take great faith to stand in confidence and say before God's people, *"Thus saith the Lord!"*

When God told me to do it, I did. God proved Himself to be the One behind my words. He was speaking on my behalf and that's when my faith was called into question. Not only my faith but my intentions because to them God would not call someone as young as me without any credentials, very little finance, a hand full of faithful members, to lead them into a place where very few had gone in such a short amount of time. In a sense, the ability to get up in cold climates for recreational purposes developed a taste in my spirit for the impossible. Hearing God speak clearly to me made me realize that when faced with the impossible, I wouldn't be a foreigner, because I had been conditioned to lead.

DAVID'S TRIAL

Having a heart for God is an indicator that you have been trained and disciplined to commit to a life learning and mastering emotions. For those who are familiar with the life of David the young shepherd boy, he was chosen because of his heart for God. And with that came a great amount of emotional hurt and let down from people who should have known him the best. David was left out of the equation when Jesse came to the house for the anointing ceremony; his motive was questioned by his brothers at what would be his installation service when faced with Goliath. And I believe the lack of emotional stability in his childhood led him to seek emotional approval in Bathsheba the day he was in bed when he should have been at battle.

When you have the burden of transparency and extensive emotional encounters, you'll have to face it with God, not alone. I, like David, would have to learn how to master my emotions if this ministry was really going to be unique. Having faith in God does not mean that you don't want to express yourself in more elaborate terms when your motives are constantly being called into question. Especially, when the evidence is of God's favor. That simply means His favor follows wherever you go.

Favor is not fair for those who lack it, yet it is definitely fair for those who possess it. People have devised ways of making you feel guilty for being blessed, but I cannot explain any other reason for God granting His favor to this ministry except it is a byproduct of being a person after God's own heart. This special gift of favor would attract unusual attention because of the unusual anointing that comes with it. I knew people were going to doubt my ministry; preachers would underestimate my zeal; and the snakes would be bothered by my flight. I use the analogy of snakes because my greatest human fear is coming face to face with a snake. I fear them but I also study them just in case of a confrontation.

For three years, it seemed that as I did my morning workouts that there would be unusual news coming from the clouds concerning New Fellowship Church of Fort Worth. This news would be seen in how well I carried it in my behavior. I saw visions that once I mentioned to the congregation about building, that there would be a disturbance to the "snake" environment. There would be buildings erected that would move them from comfortable hunting grounds. We would experience an elevated attitude in the community that would sneak up on the snake, giving it little anticipation to strike back. And a force from on high would take over the community and the unashamed faith I had would cause me to feel as if my faith was being put on the witness stand every Sunday while I stood in the pulpit.

My now newly self-appointed enemies became the jury of my peers with a slanted agenda. Most of them did not want a pastor to shepherd them, they wanted a preacher to condone them. My unusual relationship with God created chaos to the traditional Baptist member, and it would intimidate those who were satisfied with settling for just being known as God's child. This book allows you an opportunity to sit in on a classic case of a man's faith being put on trial for trusting God, who trusted me with several people who couldn't be trusted. Throughout this trial I met my purpose while properly managing my pain and I received a great reward for the trouble.

THE MINISTRY THAT MISCARRIED

Let me talk to women real quick about how to effectively manage the pain caused by the person you love the most, be it your male counterpart, your child, loved ones, friends, or co-workers, whomever. Sister, Woman of God, first and foremost, you have to be willing to let the pain go. I know that sounds easier said than done but you have to be willing to say, "God I can't do this without you, please take this pain away." Start there and repeat it as many times and as often as you need to so you can begin the process of healing.

By no stretch of the imagination is healing from pain that simple because you still have to deal with your emotions and the feelings of hurt, rejection, fear, and so on. But you have to speak it first. The Bible says in Proverbs 18:21, *"The power of life and death are in the tongue"* and if the devil can get you to stay quiet and internalize your pain then he is winning. So utter those words that you need help from God, right now. Tell God that you are ready to release the pain that has been caused by others but most importantly the pain that has been caused by you. Yes, you can cause yourself pain when you refuse to let go and let God.

I have seen the women in my life hold onto situations and sometimes people far too long. They have shed tears from the pain that a person close to them caused them. They fought others with their words in defense of those they loved but who really wasn't ready or capable of loving them back, at least not in that moment. I have witnessed through my congregation the pain that my sisters have had to endure from men who used them for sex, money, emotional support, and other reasons but never gave back to them the way they needed that support given. These women worked daily to hide their pain from others and get into true worship and fellowship but their eyes never lied. So often I was showed the hurt and pain they were refusing to let go.

Stop right now and tell God you can't do this without Him and that you are ready to let go of the pain. Tell Him right now that you are sorry for carrying around so much deadweight that it limited your praise and weakened your faith. Forgive yourself for holding onto the misery. If God has forgiven you, then why is it so hard for you to forgive yourself? Talk to God and tell him, honestly because He already knows, He's just been waiting on you to let Him remove the pain. If you cried, then good for you. If you didn't, then give it time and keep calling out to God until you release the pain because dear Woman of God, it is time that you let go of the pain.

The reason I'm targeting women early in my book is because women you have been given the honorable task and priceless gift of bearing children. And even when you have no children you still have the power to give birth. Your hopes, dreams, goals, and aspirations will only get accomplished by how you view your pain before you give birth. From what I've gathered from the Women of God I know is that the pushing out of a child can be more difficult than the actual contractions. Pushing is painful. But pushing in the proper direction produces a beautiful baby that is worth all the pain the mother endured. You'll only give birth to your purpose if you view your pain properly.

One of my strongest adversaries who came against me was a woman. She came boldly and proclaimed that her gift from God was to expose pastors. Let's be clear, that is not a gift that the Holy Spirit would give anyone. Matter of fact, if you can produce biblical evidence that exposing pastors is a God-given gift, I will gladly eat the pages of this book. Discernment is a gift but not exposure and those two words are not the same. But again, this woman was so determined to find fault in everything that I did that she convinced herself that God placed her in the ministry to "expose" me as she said. But her desires to stand at the front of the line to persecute me had nothing to do with me. She was hurt and operating in a vicious cycle of pain.

This woman experienced pain from her husband, who at the time was incarcerated. She experienced pain from her previous pastor, who is responsible for ousted her from his church thus leading her to join with New Fellowship. When no one else would take her New Fellowship would. All her life she was rejected and mistreated by the men who she loved and at times who she needed. So pain became her comfort and the same fuel to persecute me. She was extremely vocal in her distain for me and even her allegations, even though she could produce no evidence. To make matters worse she was the church treasurer and when rumors began to surface that I was stealing money from our bank loan she was there holding the books but couldn't produce a single piece of evidence that showed that I was guilty. She kept the checks in her possession and she signed off on them. That was our system, that the checks issued by the church needed two signatures.

How ironic that the woman who controlled the church funds accused me of stealing money that I did not have access to? But she did because she lived out her pain daily and I was next in line because I was her new pastor. She had been hurt by her former pastor, abandoned by the one before him, hurt by an inconsistent husband, and because of these untamed emotions, her ministry could not produce. She was extremely gifted but mismanaged her pain which led to a spiritual miscarriage.

How many of you women have persecuted innocent men in your lives because of the pain you refuse to let go of? Take a minute to think about the times you lashed out in anger at a man, be they an adult or child, because of something they did that reminded you of someone who hurt you. I know this is a hard exercise but I am trying to get you to move past your pain and into your healing. Pain is inevitable and it's real but how long you hold onto it is determined only by you. It's time to let God take that pain away from you. It's time to seek God for more than a blessing but for a powerful life changing move that will take you to your next level, because remember every new level we accomplish in Christ is a new level of pain. The degree in which we experience it is completely up to us and it becomes harder when we refuse to let go of past pains that cause us to bear false witness against those who were called into our lives.

Now let's begin this journey of how God picked me out, set me up, and broke me for something that I could not and had no desire to do on my own. I told God to use me and I meant every word that I uttered when I laid with God in continual prayer. I still get met with opposition and difficulty but this building process grew me to be a stronger man of God, a stronger and better husband and father and the leader God said I was without the desires to prove it.

Faith facts are things that I learned while going through my trial. I decided to include lessons that I learned during the building process of New Fellowship. That's why I decided to share my faith facts with you and help you learn more about your faith. At the end of each chapter I will have Faith Facts and then I will challenge you to increase your faith in God.

CHAPTER 1

PRE-TRIAL MOTION

"Now faith is the substance of things hoped for, the evidence of things not seen." Hebrews 11:1 KJV

In our lives we all experience working with our own personal Saul. Saul is that person, leader, manager, friend or family member who seeks to destroy us regardless of how good we treat them or how good we make them look with our own personal best efforts. Early in my career as a minister I encountered my own personal Saul. My Saul did not come until I finally answered the call of God to preach to another man's sheep. It was a time in my life, though I didn't realize it at that particular time, that God was preparing me to be falsely accused and even convicted by those who called me to lead them as their pastor. My Saul days prepared me for my days of relentless persecution. My, my, my … the awesomeness of God, that He cared enough for me to prepare me for the longest trial of my life.

Don't think I accepted the call to pastor with my hands up, surrendering it all to God. No, it was quite the opposite. I came with a chip on my shoulder. I wanted to show anyone who would look and listen that I was truly the man of God that they believed was called to lead them. That chip on my shoulder made me pray harder, dive deeper in my Word, and live in God's presence from the time I woke up to the time I went to bed. I was determined to be all and more of who God called me to be. The expectations I had for myself were different than most and during my Saul days I often felt ignored and rejected by my leader. What are Saul days? Those were the days in which I was assigned to serve in a ministry where the leadership was questionable, at best. I had to learn to observe, listen, accept criticism, and serve in silence. He (Saul) treated me as if I was the enemy because of God's expectation on my life. God has always had something different in store for me … something different and grand to do. My only job was to be obedient and continue to be who he called me … different.

THE SEASON I SERVED SAUL

The season I served "Saul" I experienced a lot of things that would have turned many new preachers away. But for me it sparked a desire to help people heal even more who had been hurt by this man or any other person in their lives for that matter. All my life, including as a pastor, I saw how traditional religion and its practices hurt people. Traditional religion being the rules and regulations of a certain church such as what to wear, how you need to conduct yourself and other nuances that separated the people who faithfully practiced the rules of church from the people who truly sought a relationship with the true and living God. These people gave, worshipped, and lived their lives as if it were scripted because old time religion said to do so. They were devoted, maybe not to God, but to the practices and rules that were set by their assigned or elected leader. I was the same way. I had "religious rules" that I had lived by my entire Christian life because it was how I was raised and early in my pastoral career I dared not stray away from these traditions.

But as God used me and enlarged my heart and my thinking, He also enabled me to break away from the rules of traditional religion. I no longer desired to be the same as others because I asked God to use me outside of my comfort zone and beyond my own understanding. I was determined to be more than a pastor with the ability to preach. I wanted to help people break away from the pain they were experiencing including the pain from the church, their pastors, the religious traditions they had learned so early in their lives. I had a desire to be separated from others because I was different; I was made by God for a specific reason, just like you.

Under the leadership of my previous pastor, I was oftentimes treated as if I were his personal adversary. As if I had ulterior motives and wanted to take over the ministry he was leading. I do admit that I always knew that I was going to lead my own church but I thought that the leading that I was going to do would be out of my home with my wife. I never wanted to lead my former pastor's congregation because I knew the pain that he put them through I would inherit. I can't tell you how many times I wanted to break free from him and run away but God told me to stay in position, to be still. You can only imagine how difficult it is to stay still, to stay in position, when you want to leave a situation before something bad happens.

He, I do apologize for not giving a name but the relevance is to minister to you and not to call names and focus any attention on the negative, would stand in front of the congregation and literally call people out who he felt were against him. I stayed frustrated at the audacity and arrogance of this man. When I began to minister in his church and my popularity increased he treated me as one who wanted to be a minister for selfish reasons. He was bold enough to take jabs at me while giving his sermons and he was successful, during my time there, in keeping me away from ministering at other churches as a visiting preacher. I didn't find that out until I left and it hurt that he talked about me even though I continued to lift his name up as an upstanding man of God.

You may have prayed for God to use you, to deliver you or even for Him to give you strength but because Satan is so crafty, he causes utter chaos in your life, leaving you wanting to do one thing ... leave. The Bible tells us in Isaiah 40:30-31, *"Even youths grow tired and weary, and young men stumble and fall; but those who hope in the Lord will renew their strength. They will soar on wings like eagles; they will run and not grow weary, they will walk and not be faint."* But when God gives you an order, especially one to be still, take heed and be obedient because your blessings and the blessings of others always lie at the other end of your struggles. I want you to remember this ... the answer you don't want to hear is usually the answer that is coming directly from God.

BEING PUT ON TRIAL

When I received my call to pastor, I had absolutely no history of pastoring or leading others, in a congregational setting. My past was spotty because I was a former street pharmacist, a.k.a. drug dealer, and I had my pick and share of women but I also had a heart for God. I know it sounds contradictory but didn't God change Moses, Peter, David and so many others in the Bible who had the worst past mistakes? But God still placed His favor upon them, just like He does when He picks someone to make a change in the masses. For me, my lack of history as a pastor even made those in the pastor community believe that I wasn't ready to pastor because I didn't have enough experience as a pastor to lead a church, to speak to the lost or, to even write this book on faith.

As I look back over all the trials and tribulations during my career as a pastor, I realized that I was being put on trial by God. I was being setup by the God Himself for a purpose that was to not only free the people I was called to lead but to free myself from the prison that I had put myself in. So just for a minute let's imagine being in a courtroom where you are preparing to go before the judge. You have never committed the crime you are being accused of but yet you are sitting in the courtroom preparing to defend yourself against false accusations that you have no evidence to counter. You have witnesses who can vouch for your character as well as your whereabouts but their testimonies cannot be used in court because they, like you, have a "past" that most would consider questionable. How would you feel knowing that these people can get you off the hook and have all the charges dropped but their testimonies are worthless because they don't fit the bill for being a model Christian?

I was touted as being the underdog because that's who I wanted to be. I wanted to be the person who could prove everyone wrong and make their jaw drop. It gave me pleasure knowing that I changed someone's opinion or belief about me. I approached every aspect of my life like that. My role as the underdog was written before I was born. All of my life I was considered a nobody and I was often counted out before I ever got a chance to prove myself. I was usually the shortest in the group but I excelled in other areas despite my height. That made me fight even harder to prove everyone wrong. That passion was instilled in me early on in my childhood. I believed that I always had to prove my self-worth to others because I was shorter and smaller. For some having the feeling of "I've got to prove myself" can be detrimental but for me it was actually a self-discipline tool that would be the very thought pattern that made me endure in difficult situations. I found that believing when there was no evidence, hoping when there was no hope and weathering the storms of being a leader were the perfect conditions for being put on trial by God. I had to be an underdog because it was the only way God could truly get the glory out of every encounter and for His children to understand that He is the great I AM.

Sometimes in your life you have to be the underdog-the person who is always counted out and never called on. God does His best works with underdogs. That's when God knows that with you and through you He can receive the praise and the glory even during your storm. It's okay to be counted out because as a leader and child of the Most High God you know who to count on.

BEING THE UNDERDOG

I truly believed that I had to be the underdog including being short in stature. Being an underdog is not a bad trait, if you use it for its God-given purpose. An underdog is a person or group who is/are popularly expected to lose. The party, team, or individual expected to win is called the favorite or top dog. In the rare case where an underdog wins, the outcome is an upset. The use of the term is believed to have come from the blood-sport known as bear-baiting where the "top dog" was trained to attack the bear's throat and head, and the "underdog" was trained to attack the bear's underside. The top dog had a better chance of surviving and of beating the bear, whereas the underdog was most likely to die.

God didn't give me height but He sure did give heart! My height caused me to be rejected a lot and eventually that rejection became the emotion responsible for stirring up my determination. So the more I was rejected the more I fought and sought to provide a righteous outcome for those who were just like me. I wanted all of us "underdogs" to drink from the cup of victory and that was my motivation and the rejection I received was the fuel for my faith. I believe that if I had never been underestimated or rejected early in my life then I would not have developed the drive to survive in adverse circumstances.

It wasn't until June 1, 2006 where I would answer the call to become the ultimate underdog, assigned to this task by God. I was asked to become the pastor of New Fellowship Church during a time when most pastors were being chosen by their degrees and longevity to become pastor of an already established ministry. I had no church, I had little training, but I was still chosen. Let me say that again so you can understand how God uses the underdog … I had no church, I had little training, but I was still chosen. And while I thought I would be the last person they would consider to become their pastor, I was the perfect person to become their pastor. To me, I was the perfect person to exact change because I was born into a neighborhood where competition was unending.

As a young boy my friends and I would compete over everything. We competed about who could get to the end of the street the fastest; who could drink their soda first; who could be the first to the bus stop in the morning ... anything that warranted being the first, we engaged in competition over it. Because of this playful competitive spirit that I had with my friends, I ultimately got involved in sports. To this day, I consider myself to be a pretty athletic person but the one thing that kept me competing against my friends and then my teammates, was the fact that I was determined to prove to them and myself that even though I was shorter, I belonged there. I didn't realize that I creating passion that God was going to use later in my life.

These scriptures burned in me through the years, 1 Samuel 16:7 (NIV) *But the Lord said to Samuel, "Do not consider his appearance or his height, for I have rejected him. The Lord does not look at the things people look at. People look at the outward appearance, but the Lord looks at the heart."*

1 Samuel 16:12 (NIV) *So he sent for him and had him brought in. He was glowing with health and had a fine appearance and handsome features. Then the Lord said, "Rise and anoint him; this is the one."*

We all know that being tall is a symbol authority, power, and strength. Having a Greek-god like stature always points victory or being an overachiever. And many churches seek to place the poised tall man into position. But the danger in that when it comes to traditional Baptist churches is that they seek the good looks and height while failing to investigate the heart. But didn't David slay Goliath? The underdog killed the top dog, all because he continuously allowed God to search his heart so he could be used by God. There are other underdogs in history:

- Boxer James "Buster" Douglas, given odds of 42:1 by one Las Vegas sports book, handed the previously-undefeated Mike Tyson his first ever professional defeat in Tokyo, Japan on February 11, 1990. This was the largest upset in the history of boxing.

- U.S. President Harry Truman in the 1948 presidential election was considered the underdog but was elected into office.

- In Super Bowl XLII, the New York Giants defeated the New England Patriots 17-14. The Patriots had gone the season undefeated.

- In Super Bowl III, the New York Jets, led by quarterback Joe Namath, defeated the heavily-favored Baltimore Colts 16-7 after giving a "guarantee" to do so.

There are so many instances of hope when it comes to being the underdog. In these examples these underdogs made history. But in cases concerning the kingdom, underdogs point to God's glory. I say that because there is no way to explain how a church with less than three years of history and 70 members, at the time, can prepare to build a facility just under a million dollars during a recession. Fortunately, we had enough faith walkers to help us achieve the possible during a season of so many impossibilities.

When Samuel went to Jesse's house in Bethlehem to anoint the next king, it was a shepherd name David who would be appointed. Unfortunately, no one knew enough of him nor didn't they believe in him, not even his own parents and brothers. He was selected to be king but he was the underdog. Can you imagine living in a home where not one person thought you would be anything more than what they saw? David was a shepherd. Who are you? Maybe no one thought enough of you outside of being the little runt of the group or the person that stayed to themself or even the one that everyone talked bad about. That's exactly what happened to David and what I experienced throughout my life.

Saul was chosen by the Israelites to be their king on looks and stature, not character. During his reign he proved to be a suspect concerning spiritual things, a man of questionable motives, and at times moments of schizophrenia. When you choose anyone before checking their history thoroughly, it can prove to be very costly. We comb through the backgrounds of people in the corporate world, but in this case the church we fail to do a divine background check with God about things we want in right now moments. Saul hurt Israel to its core and didn't care that he did it because he felt justified. In my life, there have been "Sauls" who pastored before me and who hurt the people who I would eventually be elected to lead. I faced so many struggles because the people failed to forgive their Sauls so they made me responsible for leading them down the path of righteousness, even though they were unwilling to go.

PREPARING FOR TRIAL

When God gave me the order to build our current facility, it was June 1, 2008 at 5 a.m. I was doing what I had always done on Sunday mornings before church – a 3-mile run at North Crowley Middle School track. On this particular Sunday, this workout would change my life permanently. I kept hearing God say, *"Upon this rock I will build my church,"* but what I understood by build my church and God's meaning of build my church were the exact opposite. I thought God wanted me to start pastoring the members more frequently but God was saying build a place so I can come in and worship. We were using ran down buildings with rats and other creatures, holes in the roof and electrical issues. I thought we needed to secure a storefront location which was tailor made for smaller ministries like ours. Again, nowhere near what God had on His mind.

I know that in order to build the body of believers it would not only require a pastor but a dramatic change of perception. And anyone with a taste for the dramatic understands that there is a performance that goes on behind the scenes of ministry. I had to learn to deal with presuppositions and critical darts because of how some had been treated by their former leaders, family members and friends. People's negative perception of you can be the stumbling block that causes you to lose hope in what you believe in. If you listen to negativity and criticism long enough, then you'll begin to question yourself. So as I prepared to build according to God's idea of building, I had to prepare myself for some doubts and attacks, but I didn't realize that no amount of preparation could have prepared me for what I was about to endure when I stood in the pulpit and told the church that God told me to build us a church.

Before I got the chance to change the culture of the church and heighten the awareness of those who had been in charge, I had to go through a series of trials to prove my character. When I said we were going to build a new facility for us to worship in, they only heard I, Patrick Diggs, wanted to build a church to prove myself better than their former leadership. Every word that God convicted me to say, they heard coming from me and not from God. I didn't realize that that moment was the start of the evidence gathering each member would partake in. Everything I did and said from that moment on would be compiled against me and used to shake and destroy my faith. They quickly started thinking that I had my own selfish agendas. But I knew I was being led by God and God alone because I truly had absolutely no desires to build my own church. My reasoning was because I had watched the hardships of their former pastor build the church and I knew without a shadow of a doubt that I did not want to be bothered with that mess.

Keep in mind that they called on me to be their pastor. I was always anointed by God to preach, just not when they appointed me, so they thought. I had been God's choice for them before I was conceived in my mother's womb. I understood this but it would take some time for me to get them to understand it. So the best way I could convince them that I was really a man of God was to prove it through my faith. There was a chaos that God was calling me to calm. That's the one thing I understood from growing up in church. I knew that the lack of order that's often within today's churches is God's M.O. No, he does not deal in confusion, that's Satan, but God deals with divine order and being selected to pastor New Life was God's perfect order of bring resolution to a lost flock.

When I took the call of leading, I inherited people who had money to give but no cause to give it to. They were rich in finance put poor in faith. There is such thing as having faith to begin a project but not having the faith to believe in the project to its completion. That led them to collectively adopting a crippling philosophy that people in the church leadership should be appointed before the leader is anointed. Unfortunately, history has taught us that there is very little use for anything that is crippled. You can't be as effective as you want to be by being crippled in any area of your life. If you think negatively all the time, then you are crippled in your thoughts. If you have sometime belief, then you are crippled in your faith. If you talk bad against others all the time, then you are crippled in your speech. You can't go far being crippled but God can still use you because everything and everyone God uses is prepared first.

When you read the Bible you will discover that the men and women who accomplished great things for God weren't content with accepting the status quo. They believed that more could be done if and only if someone would lead the way. And when no one else stepped forward to lead, they themselves volunteered. Talk about a desire to be used by God. I was called when no one else stepped forward. I will admit that it took some time before I answered the call to build because the more I ignored it the message rang louder in my ears. This ringing rang so loudly that even my wife began to hear it. And after much prayer and fasting we were confident God wanted us to step out on faith and build the church.

Now, when you look at what I just wrote in a spiritual manner it looks something like this: The life of faith is inherently a life of risk. Go back to your Bible and take a moment to look at the men and women who did great things for God. Almost without exception, they were risk takers who weren't afraid to lay it all on the line for God. Consider these examples of the men and women of the Bible who allowed God to use them:

- Noah built an ark
- Abraham left Ur of the Chaldees to go to the Promised Land
- Moses led the people of God out of Egypt

- Joshua marched around the walls of Jericho
- David defeated Goliath
- Elijah faced down the prophets of Baal
- Esther risked everything to save her people
- Daniel refused to defile himself with the king's food
- Nehemiah led the Jews to rebuild the walls of Jerusalem

All of these people allowed themselves to be used by God. They had radical faith even in times of certain death or failure and from that radical faith God was able to use them to produce radical results for the people they were called to lead. You have to have that same radical faith and belief in God that He can and will use you to lead people who are in pain. It is apparent that the Lord works in mysterious ways. There, I said it. The way He works to get His will done in our lives can seem so backwards, counter-intuitive, and at times controversial but when we live by faith and not by sight, His will will be done.

The Bible is filled with divine order when it comes to starting and building a church. That order is God anoints and appoints the man and then the people follow him. Unfortunately, many churches believe that the people have the right to appoint the leader without him or her ever being anointed. When you operate in this way of thinking, you will always be tested. I was anointed by God but appointed by the people. When they called me to lead them I went to God and He gave me the permission to move forward. Again, I was anointed to preach even though they appointed me to lead so when God said move forward, I didn't realize that it would blow my mind.

I was being led into the slaughter house, into the furnace, if you will, to be set up for my faith. I understand, now, that I needed to be on trial for my faith and even then I was willing to allow those who prosecuted me to investigate everything I did until they were satisfied. Unfortunately, their hate and distain for me would not allow them to be satisfied with what they found because God always proved my innocence. I was not building the church for my glory but rather for my desires to follow God and for His glory. Despite the accusations that I was stealing money, I showed repeatedly that the money I earned from my job and from the ministry from preaching was being sowed back into the ministry. My character was constantly questioned because the general contractor, who was referred to me by some of the members, was stealing money and our equipment, yet in still I prayed for him when he came before the church for prayer. I was determined to let my faith be used as evidence in my own trial.

Like Jeremiah18-20 (NIV) the Lord revealed to me that they had a plot to ruin me and if at all possible cause their distain and hatred for me to kill me. I had former members pull guns out on me because they were convicted that they were right in their persecutions of my character. This scripture truly ministered to my soul because I knew that I was assigned, appointed and anointed by God and God alone. *"Because the Lord revealed their plot to me, I knew it, for at that time he showed me what they were doing. I had been like a gentle lamb led to the slaughter; I did not realize that they had plotted against me, saying, "Let us destroy the tree and its fruit; let us cut him off from the land of the living, that his name be remembered no more." But you, Lord Almighty, who judge righteously and test the heart and mind, let me see your vengeance on them, for to you I have committed my cause."* Imagine God himself protecting you against those who bear false witness and rise up against His will.

A CALL TO ORDER

When building anything, especially buildings, the foundation is extremely critical. The architect would be a failure if he began to build an infrastructure based on miscalculating the weight, height, and stress the project would be able to handle beforehand. Just like an architect you have to build a solid foundation of faith. This building process is not easy because Satan seeks, in every waking moment, to destroy your faith in God so you can turn against God. Your faith needs to be the very foundation that allows you to bend but not break because bending allows you to be stretched by God but not broken by the devil. I am convinced that whenever God builds a church Satan build a chapel nearby.

In Matthew 17:20, Jesus said, *"Truly I tell you, if you have faith as small as a mustard seed, you can say to this mountain, 'Move from here to there,' and it will move. Nothing will be impossible for you."* This is evidence that your faith is the most important thing that you possess and Satan is always seeking to destroy it, especially when you answer the call of God.

At the beginning of any new project or journey, there will always be a need for order. In the business world a person who brings about order to a new project is called a project manager. Though it's a much needed task in the corporate and government sectors, the church constantly rejects a leader whose main objective is to do things in an orderly fashion. Order and opposition are bunkmates when dealing with people who just love going to church. I was met with that rejection and opposition but I was determined to prove to them that by walking as close to God as I could, that I was indeed on a divine appointment.

I'd like to pause for a moment and encourage young pastors that if you have a vision or a desire to start a ministry, then know that it is the most difficult and daunting task you will ever experience. In other words, IT'S NOT ALL IT'S CRACKED UP TO BE!

There will be days when you will want to act how you're being treated. Then there will be times when you want to give up. There will be other times when you will feel like getting in your car and driving as far as you can and never coming back. The only thing that will prevent you from doing any, if not all of these things, is by remembering who you work for and that *our present sufferings are not worth comparing with the glory that will be revealed in us.* (Romans 8:18, NIV).

As I go through this story of my faith being put on trial, I'd like to offer some principles here to help you understand how important having a promise from God is. I had an experience similar to the one a servant girl named Hagar did in Genesis 15-

16. Abram obeyed God and was given a promise to become the father of many nations (Gen. 12:2). It goes on to say that in the latter part of verse 3 *"And all families that come from you will be blessed."*

During this time of Hagar's life she gets put out of the house with her son Ishmael. As she sits under a tree and cries out to God, the Lord hears the cry of the boy. That is very significant. It does not say he heard the cry of Hagar but he heard the boy. Meaning God answered the cry of the boy because the boy came from the loins of Abram. Even when it looks like the promise has been compromised, God will still honor the promise He made to your mother, father, aunts, uncles or your great great great grandparents. Like Hagar, her son was okay because the boy came from Abram and the promise was made on behalf of Abram. So if you were to lose everything you have, make sure your faith remains intact because you have everything you need from God to start all over again.

During my season of tribulation, I always remembered how God kept His word even when I lacked the strength to wait on Him. This should help you stand when no one else is standing by your side that the God we serve is just and stands with us, always. Your faith should be fortified and reassured that everything and everyone else will fail you but God will not. If you have ever felt wronged for doing what you knew in your heart was right, then don't worry because there are biblical accounts about people who felt alone or disheartened during the trial of their faith – Jesus, being the most prominent biblical figure, was persecuted and executed for His faith. The one thing I had to learn and I hope you learn as well, is that when life puts you in a predicament to where God is all you've got, that's when you'll discover that God is all you need.

If you remember nothing else, then please remember these two things that you should refer back to as you study and learn more about having your faith on trial:

1. Remember God's promise.
2. His promise must be kept.

Such is the case with Job. A man who prayed without ceasing, sacrificed burnt offerings before God, brought in the tithe and then some, yet for some strange reason he lost everything that was precious to him. But the one thing that remained was his faith in God and from his faith in God he was restored. Job had a choice, he could have cursed God and died because he was sick and afflicted so long that even his own flesh was falling from his bones. Job openly confessed, *"Though He slay me, the angels deliberate, Satan instigates, Heaven hesitates, and then God communicates."*

Job had gotten so defeated in his own darkness that he lost faith in himself but never in God. Fortunately for Job, God showed favor and mercy on him and delivered Job from his affliction once he humbled himself and prayed for his friends. He was restored and received double for what he lost, which included 7,000 sheep, 3,000 camel, 500 oxen, and 500 donkeys and the restoration of his children and wife.

We have to have the faith and conviction to know that if we stand on the promises of God that we will receive double for our troubles.

FAITH FACT

Faith is so vital to the life of a Christian to where God Himself declares it is impossible to please Him without it.

1. What are some things that you do to increase your faith in God?
2. Have you been called to lead a project on your job or start a new journey in your life? If so, then list out the pros and cons of moving forward.
3. How often do you talk, praise or pray to God during your day?

CHAPTER 2

THE MISUNDERSTOOD JURY

"And when I came to you, brethren, I did not come with superiority of speech or of wisdom, proclaiming to you the [a]testimony of God. For I determined to know nothing among you except Jesus Christ, and Him crucified." I Corinthians 2:1-2 (NASB)

Evidence of things hoped for became my mantra. It was the one thing that sustained me. I started to learn during the process of building our new church that there were two groups of people that I ministered to, those who were bitter and those who were becoming better. When you deal with a bitter person, it's like trying to help a venomous snake. You know it's poisonous and it could kill you but you still try to help it nonetheless because of who you are. Matter of fact, there is a fable that I heard when I was a child about a woman who picked up a snake, took it home and nursed it back to health. When the snake got better it lashed out and bit the woman. Before she died she told the snake that she was surprised that it bit her and its answer was simple … "You knew I was a snake when you took me in." That's how bitter people are. They know they are bitter but they oftentimes they bite those who genuinely want to help. Eventually, like the snake, they lash out and their bitterness kills (not literally) the person who was just trying to help. Has your bitterness caused you to hurt people who are trying to help you?

That other group of people included those who have allowed certain situations and conditions in their lives to cause them so much pain and misery. This group of people usually doesn't know how to escape or leave so they hold it in and that's where the bitterness starts to fester. Some of the members of the church I inherited were like that, they wanted to leave the previous ministry but didn't know how to or couldn't so they slowly started to erode spiritually and emotionally. I just became their target because I was sent to help them. Fortunately, this group can be turned around because they constantly fight, pray, and struggle with going to the dark side.

I hate to use another analogy but it helps to understand the points I am making if I relate it to something real. In the movies Star Wars Luke, the main character, has a constant struggle with the 'Dark Side' because of who his father is. He struggles to know if he is a good guy or a bad guy and eventually that struggle starts to consume him and he begins to lash out at those who were on the journey with him, his friends. Fortunately, Luke prevails because he remembers his teachings, had faith, and his friends were constant but some of us don't have what Luke had and that's how bitterness takes over. Do you feel like you are constantly struggling to find your way?

What I have learned as a pastor is that when you try to get people to break away from the traditions of religion, it is undoubtedly a difficult feat. It's difficult and sometimes damaging because people don't want to change what they have been taught for so many years. Religion is a compilation of practices, rules, and ordinances and in the Baptist church, one of the most famed religious practices is the members' ability to oust their leader if they believe, without evidence, wrongdoing is taking place. For my situation, the wrongdoing that had taken place was with the previous pastor, not me, and because they failed to act against him they sought and succeeded in persecuting me.

I was on trial for his sins and their inability to do anything about it for three long years. Again, he stole from them, made light of their hardships, and ridiculed them in public. He hid things from them and challenged anyone who challenged him. So when I changed that practice under my leadership and started an open door policy, the reception of hope I thought I would receive was met with scorn and accusations of false motives because of their previous religious beliefs. They were determined, and consistent, to make me pay for his sins. As I began to realize that I was paying for his sins, I started to feel as if I had followed God to a dead end. And that's where bitterness started to become my companion.

FOLLOWING TO A DEAD END

What is God up to? Have you ever asked yourself that when you realize that you are facing a dead end situation after following God? I asked that question, as did my wife, several times during those three years. It was a constant question for me and to my wife. What is God up to? Why is He silent now? What did I do to deserve leading these people? The questions were plentiful and endless because I wanted to know why I was at a dead end, or at least felt like I was at a dead end on a mission that God had appointed me to. I recalled the Israelites who were leaving Egypt following Moses who was following God. Initially they were exiting to the Southeast of Egypt but God changed their direction to go to the south.

God led them not through the way of the land of the Philistines, although that was near; for God in Exodus 13:7said,

"Lest peradventure the people repent when they see war and they return to Egypt."

The reason God changed their path is simple. They would have encountered a war in the land of the Philistines which would have caused them to lose heart and maybe even their lives. Eventually they came before the Red Sea and that's when things looked like it was the end. Pharaoh's army was behind them and the Red Sea was in front of them. They had nowhere to go, so they thought. Have you ever wondered how many times God has stalled you or turned you around to keep you from losing heart or even your life? Sometimes when we stand for God, He puts us into just the right place for Him to show who He is. God placed me in just the right place, the pulpit, to stand and deliver a message of redemption and hope to those who needed a shepherd but really did not want one. Like Moses I was now faced with my own Red Sea, answering the call to build a new church while everything around us was starting to go to pieces. We had ragged building, naysayers in- and outside of the church, no land or money, and to top it all off in front of us the call to build a new facility.

To make matters worse, the key people in the church also answered a call, just not a righteous one. They were called, answered, and accepted the call to undermine the man of God they appointed as their leader. My persecutors attempted daily to deliver nothing but confusion. They were relentless and oftentimes gathered together after I had finished preaching, waiting for me or my wife to exit, so we could see them talking about us. I can only imagine what their conversations were about but the torment of them was unbearable some days. Especially those days when I had just bared my soul to the Lord and gave the congregation my best.

I knew that if I was going to be on trial, I was going to be on trial representing God to the fullest. Remember, I am the underdog so my decision to stand firm on God's word and prove that I was a man of God was embedded in me. I was going to fight regardless if I wanted to because it's all I had conditioned myself to do. When that adoration they had in the beginning turned into hatred, it added to the pain and that is something that I will never forget.

Over time I have learned to forgive those who sought to destroy my character, my name, and at times even tested my faith in myself as their pastor. That's why I decided to write this book about the faith because I had to understand how to discover the fullness and closeness I would need to have with God and to not let the bitterness of this experience hold me back from being a blessing and receiving my blessings. My journey about having my faith placed on trial for three years is a true testament of my God-given purpose to lead people who were in pain. So let the pages of this book will help you properly manage the pain in your life, especially after you have been chosen by God or even people, but are then persecuted for having the faith to continue to move forward. God doesn't make mistakes so when He puts you where you are, whether it's currently, in the past or coming soon, then know... it's always for a greater purpose than you can ever imagine. Pain is inevitable when you trust and believe God with everything you are and everything you know, even when it doesn't make sense to anyone else not even you.

You will have people who will work tireless to find evidence against you for their own selfish gain. I firmly believe that the plan of my persecutors to start the church was motivated by proving others wrong. The verbal, emotional, and financial abuse they endured from their former pastor would have caused them to find fault in any man of God, I was just the one God chose to use. God needed this assignment, journey, whatever you want to call it to break me before I could free them. Thank God He chose me because He had growth on His mind and change in His plan for the church as well as for me. The hurt of having money being mishandled, the appearance of extramarital affairs, and other corruptible things from the former pastor fell on my shoulders and they were determined to make me, my wife, and the church pay for it.

For years, while I was under the same leadership that my persecutors were under, I stared to hear God tell me things. I knew one thing that I wanted to leave where I was many times but God told me to be still. I hated that part but again I didn't know that God was preparing me for the battle that was just around the corner with the same people. I had to not only fight with the pastor, but I had to fight with bitterness, anger, and resentment because I was being abused while serving God faithfully. The members were hurt, they were suffering at the hands of what they called a so-called man of God ... they were just a mess emotionally and their hatred for him ultimately spilled over to me. They had been abused so much so that it was normal for them to receive criticism and hateful remarks from their leader. They expected it and honestly I believe they secretly craved it because it kept excitement in their bitter lives. His constant taunting became like clockwork under his leadership and it had no boundaries, not even within his own personal affairs.

From what I experienced it seemed that his motives were never right. I do believe that at one point, when he initially came to preach at the church that he had every intention of being a good steward but something in him changed. Again, I can't speak to what changed in him but when I was under his leadership what I saw was a corrupted man doing whatever he wanted, at the total disregard of God and his members. But what I also saw were members who were also allowing themselves to be mistreated in the name of religion. Not in the name of God but religion because for them questioning the pastor was nothing like questioning God.

That leads me to this point, when your motives for doing things you said that God called you to do aren't pure, the truth will be revealed through a series of strange tests that will eventually expose you for the fraud you are. The old pastor a.k.a. Saul was not a good leader which caused the members to become not so good members. They believed their money was able to buy whomever and whatever they wanted. Their desires lacked to receive the fullness of God. They harbored hate and anger and rejected God's love. They took religion to their graves and probably never got to have a rich and full relationship with God. I've had to bury my persecutors not only in my thoughts but also in the grave because they refused to see who God called me to be in their lives. They only saw the hate that they allowed to develop from the bitterness they failed to pray away.

UNITED WE STAND, DIVIDED WE FALL

One Sunday in 2011, I preached a sermon entitled United We Stand or Divided We Fall from Psalms 133:1-2, how good and pleasant it is when God's people live together in unity! It is like precious oil poured on the head, running down on the beard, running down on Aaron's beard, down on the collar of his robe. The purpose of this sermon was to encourage the church to stand together and worship in unity, which we did not do. In fact, we did the exact opposite. We stood in divided, and disconnected. We refused to come together and soon, as the church grew, it became us against them. Us being the new members who knew nothing of the bad blood that was brewing in the church.

Today, we live in the age of division from denomination, to splits in the church, to high rates of divorce rate … it seems that everyone is breaking up and tearing each other down. One of the most awful consequences of sin is that it makes us creatures of war. We fight instead of find solutions. Persecute instead of learn the facts. It's an unfortunate human condition that Satan thrives off of. Don't believe me? Look at the brothers Cain and Abel, who were the first examples in the Bible of warfare. Cain was so bitter towards Able to where the bitter seeds turned to cold blooded murder. How many times have you allowed your anger to go uncheck, to where it festered and your reactions caused more damage than you imagined? How long will you allow yourself to be torn from a loved one, spouse, friend or family member because of an argument? It's time to stop giving Satan energy.

Warfare is a big problem. But the question that I often ponder is, 'can we, as the body of believers, be unified?' If so, how can we learn to be unified and love as Christ loves the church? I know we can be unified but as we built the church, division was the only thing that we had in common and it took a toll on me. I prayed to God daily saying to him that we should be unified. I told myself that Jesus prayed for unity, 'I do not ask in behalf of these alone, but for those also who believe in me through their word; that they may all be one; even as Thou, Father, art in Me and I in Thee, that they also may be in Us; that the world may believe that Thou didst send Me.' (John 17:20-22) But I was getting nowhere in the church. The closer we got to getting something else approved for building the church the more divided we became and the more the pressure started to build in me that we were falling apart instead of standing together.

Unity is necessary if we are going to call ourselves the people of God. We would expect siblings to dwell together in unity. After all, they share the same nurturing system because they have the same parents. They live at the same address and eat at the same table so it would only be wise to believe that they would be unified. I know we can dispute this but let's be honest, how many times have we heard about sibling rivalry and asked ourselves, 'didn't they grow up in the same house?' We also would expect God's people to dwell together in unity – but not uniformity. God does not want uniformity among His children, He wants unity. I couldn't get the church unified but they were willing to be uniformed as it pertained to learned traditions and religion. They fought with me constantly and consistently. They caused so much warfare in the house of God that it became unbearable. Other members and I only wanted unity but then we only wanted peace, especially me. I wanted peace from it all.

For God, He wants us to have unity in society, family, workplace, and even at church. Where there is unity, there is power. To be in agreement and unified with your fellow believers is the most peaceful and powerful place for a Christian. Satan is well aware of that and he knows that if any two of us on earth agree in the name of Jesus concerning what we ask, it shall be done for us. And, where two or more are gathered together in Jesus' name, He will be there also (Matt. 18:19-20). Therefore, Satan's desire is to ruin our relationships with each other by sowing strife among us. If he can keep us in turmoil with our brothers and sisters in Christ, then he knows we will be vulnerable and lack God's power. We must, by faith, choose to abandon these negative thoughts and learn to say, not my will, but yours, as Jesus did in Matt. 26:39.

When the body of believers constantly attack one another, sow discord, fail, or refuses to forgive, fail to follow the commandments, then God smells the stench. I witnessed so many of the so-called Christians in our church say they love Jesus but fought against me and the belief that we were instructed to build the church. I often wondered how can you love a God that you cannot see but hate the man that you elected to preach and minister to you? They saw me daily, had open access to me because I lived a transparent life, and were able to talk to me about anything in complete and utter confidence and confidentiality. I was an open book and they knew it, yet when they couldn't find any evidence against me to persecute me in front of the church, it angered them.

Your enemies will become enraged when your record shows your steps are ordered by God. My steps and my actions were ordered by God and because I was determined to prove it to them I continually added more fuel to their fire. When you stand bold on the word of God your enemies will come together to attack you. There's no doubt in my mind that Satan picks and chooses carefully the people he will use to carry out his assassination plan against you. It's what he does. Remember when he was banished out of Heaven he took a third of the heavenly host of angels with him. That means he collected an army who bonded over a common agenda, to tear down the kingdom of God. If Satan did it to God, His creator, what makes you think that he won't do it to you, the person that was made in God's image?

UNITY IN UNISON

I wrote another sermon entitled, A Unified Attack. That was significant for me at the time because I was in a constant battle for my faith. Satan wanted nothing more than to destroy my faith so I could abort the mission that God had entrusted me on. Each member of Satan's appointed army had their own reason as to why they wanted me kicked out of the church as pastor. They all had their different reasons but they all had one common goal ... destroy my character and faith. When you think about having a mission aborted by Satan through your enemies you will hear many reasons but the common goal they will share is to destroy you and your faith. Think about being bullied, even if you weren't. The bullies' reasons can vary to not liking your hair, your skin color, or your clothes but the one goal they may all have is that they want to ridicule and shame you in public. That's their assignment. Like it or not.

Taking this situation biblically, I guarantee you that every last one of the Israelites had a different reason for wanting to get to the Promised Land. The main reason to get to the Promised Land was because God ordained them to do it but trust and believe me when I tell you that they all had different reasons for wanting to get there. Those reasons were revealed through their 40 years in the wilderness be they good or bad. That's why it took 40 years of wilderness because God only wanted those who were truly with His plan to crossover into the Promised Land. I relate that to the building process of NFC because we started the process in 2008 but didn't finish until 2011. Our wilderness was much shorter but by the time we entered into the building in 2011 the ones who opposed and persecuted us had disappeared. They didn't crossover into the new building even though they did come to visit, they didn't stay.

During your wilderness, rather it lasts for a day, a week, or years, the ones who oppose you the greatest and who drags you down, will not crossover into your next level unless you keep dragging them with you. Our three years of wilderness I started out being afraid to let people go who wanted to leave because I didn't want to be known as a pastor who ran off members. But over time and after time, I stopped being afraid and I was longer afraid to let them go. I eventually started wanting them to leave because they were killing me and destroying everything around me. I tell you that it's time to let 'them' go so you can hear God more and seek Him with persistence during your wilderness. I know it may be challenging or even scary but when God says move and let go, trust in Him not in them because them will keep you from God's promise.

When we purchased the land to begin building the church everyone had different reasons as to why they wanted to have a new church. For the members, they wanted better parking. The greeters wanted to a larger space that wasn't hot and crowded. The grief ministry wanted their own meeting room. The new member counselors wanted an area to properly take in new members. The finance committee wanted a larger area to count the tithes and offerings. The women's ministry wanted a place to meet. The youth department wanted a game room and classrooms. So many people had different reasons as to what they wanted out of the new building but they all wanted the new building.

Unfortunately, all of our reasons were never unified and the delays we experienced during those three years were proof. I would even venture to say that it may have been one of the reasons Satan was able to creep in and cause even more chaos because we still had our persecutors but we were adding fuel to the fire by not being on one accord.

When you do what God calls you to do, and if everybody is doing their part with joy, then everyone gets to share in the residual blessings. During any process where growth is required, there will always be people who have the perception that they are an isolated Christian. I became an isolated Christian during my trial. I worked hard, just like you maybe, to make myself believe that I didn't need so and so. I didn't need to do all of that fellowshipping. I was just going to go to church, preach, do what I do and leave. I felt like everyone around me was pretending to be unified knowing that we were slowing down.

If you're honest with yourself, then you will admit that you have been or are an isolated Christian. You may feel, right now, that you don't need to be a part of the vision or mission of your ministry. But I'm here to tell you that you very well may be holding up your own blessing. Think about it like this, what if the blessings you need will only be given by the person you are trying to avoid the most? What if you not fellowshipping or participating with the ministry or a group of people keeps you from getting that promotion, or getting the money you need to pay your bills? Your unwillingness to submit to God and His will will cause you more setbacks than you can ever imagine.

Just ask yourself, "Why did God bring me here?" There are some people around you that need to be around you because they will fight on your behalf and your righteousness. If you feel that you don't need to be around people then pray earnestly for restoration and renewal. I pray that God will remove the hardness from your heart and place you in places where you need someone that you think you don't. That way you will learn to trust God.

You have got to learn how to attack Satan in unison, with others who are for you and not against you. You can't have God's manifestation of blessings alone. Jesus only prayed alone but He worked with His team daily. I know that you've been hurt but the body of Christ needs you to be unified. There were times that I didn't believe in being unified. I just saw what I was going through. My wife was my biggest cheerleader and to this day there are some things about that time that I have not revealed to her because I thought being isolated was what I needed at the time. I am not ashamed to say that I was wrong, that's why I work hard to keep myself from that dark place because it's in the darkness that Satan takes you out.

When God has His hands on something or someone it is very important that we pay attention to His instructions. God is a God of order and when He gives orders your success depends on your attentiveness. Look at the people who you would deem successful. How do you think they achieved success? They probably paid attention to the details. When you buy anything that needs to be put together and if you don't follow the instructions correctly then something will not work or it will fall apart. If you plan on having victory in your life, then you are going to have to do it the way God said to do it, or it won't get done. There are no shortcuts or easy fixes and sometimes longsuffering is just that- a long time of suffering. But if you remember to give God the glory and to follow His instructions then weeping may endure but a night, but joy comes in the morning. You have to know that it's only a season.

Always remember that in order to serve God that He needs a unified body. He used Joshua and his army to knock down the walls of Jericho in Joshua 6:1-5, *"Now the gates of Jericho were securely barred because of the Israelites. No one went out and no one came in."* Then the Lord said to Joshua, *"See, I have delivered Jericho into your hands, along with its king and its fighting men. March around the city once with all the armed men. Do this for six days. Have seven priests carry trumpets of rams' horns in front of the ark. On the seventh day, march around the city seven times, with the priests blowing the trumpets. When you hear them sound a long blast on the trumpets, have the whole army give a loud shout; then the wall of the city will collapse and the army will go up, everyone straight in."* He went to Joshua specifically but commanded the army to march with him. God never achieves His purpose through natural means or through one person alone. Dr. Martin Luther King Jr. was given the vision but his team and others helped him execute it. Rosa Parks sat on the bus alone but the team created the change. No one is ever truly alone when the will of God must go forth. They may appear alone but God will dispatch His angels or even a complete stranger to encourage, hide, feed, or rescue.

Nothing is ever normal when God has purpose and growth on His mind. Ask yourself these questions:

- What was normal about Israel crossing the Red Sea?
- What was normal about a 16-year old teen named David taking down a 9 foot giant named Goliath?
- What's normal about being thrown into a lion's den with hungry lions and it turns into a slumber party?
- What's normal about being thrown into a fiery furnace and not being burned alive?

The Bible is filled with abnormal and unexplainable situations but the one thing that is consistent is that each of these stories had people around them. A lot of us lose ground when we complain about the assignment rather than accepting it and being obedient. Believers, including churches, who fail to follow instructions, will achieve nothing.

UNIFIED PRAISE

If you know anything about praising God, then you will understand that most of your battles can be won without you taking one swing. I had to learn this the hard way. I told you that I was known for being a man who responded with unkind words and harsh actions. I was quick to fight without knowing the details. All someone had to do was push one of the many buttons

I had and I was sure to respond. Thank God He knew more than me to keep me safe from myself. I had to learn that praise can do more fighting than I could ever do. Let me say that again but to you this time, your praise can do more than fighting can ever do for you. There's the kind of praise that you give after God has answered a prayer or came through for you. But that's just doing enough, the bare minimum, to praise only when you get your way. You have to get in the habit of praising God just for being God, to praise before and during your weak moments. Praise is not just an act of worship; it has to be a lifestyle for you.

Before the Israelites were ever freed or crossed into the Promised Land, they were instructed to praise God. Are you doing a pre-deliverance praise? From this day forward, no matter how hard it gets, no matter the road you have to travel down, that your praise has to be something you do in advance and in spite of. You have to do more than witness the praise of others but you have to engage in praise so you can move past your opposition, past the pain, and past the hurt that you have experienced in your life. I admit that there were times when I didn't want to praise or worship, yet I had to because I knew God had a promise to keep and that He wasn't going to fail me.

So like the Israelites, I was forced to give God a pre-deliverance praise, even when it hurt the most. What I discovered was that my praise was beginning to spread throughout the church and to those who were watching me handle my persecution. People who knew the kind of religious and emotional pressure I was under were wondering how I could still praise God in the midst of persecution. It was because of the faith in what I had seen beforehand. If you can't see what you don't see, then you'll never meet destiny. As I began to press my way through in praise it ignited a fire within the church that made my opposition uncomfortable. And that's when things started to turnaround for me and for others who were watching.

Always remember that with unity and unlimited praise you can began to see the possibilities in impossible situations.

FAITH FACT

The greatest time for faith to work is when sight ceases.

1. Have you really trusted that God will bring your through your toughest time?
2. The new project or journey that you just started on if you find yourself in a tough situation do you have the trust in God to wait or do you think you can take care of it immediately?
3. What are some of the discoveries you have found in your new journey that may have tried and tested your faith?

CHAPTER 3

DEFAMATION:
THE OXYMORONIC NATURE OF MINISTRY

"... but I tell you, love your enemies and pray for those who persecute you Luke." Matthew 5:44 NIV

My mother made the best cakes. Her pound cake was my favorite. I can remember like it was yesterday sitting in our living room and trying to time it perfectly when she would finish so I could ask if I could lick the cake frosting from the bowl before she washed it out. It was one of the highlights of my adolescent life. The taste of frosting after all the ingredients were mixed in was enough to keep me satisfied throughout the night. But what I never knew and what my mother never told me was that the ingredients that went into the cake before it was put into the oven would have prevented me from eating cake all together had I tried them individually.

The butter, flour, raw eggs, vanilla extract, baking powder, and vegetable oil that she used to make her cakes were not ingredients you would want to eat alone. But she needed every single ingredient because it was the only way to get the great taste that I loved. She had to bring all of those ingredients together and then put them into the hot oven for the finger licking taste that I craved. It was a process that I didn't understand until later in my life. God always has a process to get perfection out of us. Not the perfect sense, as was the case of Jesus, but the perfection of submitting to His will.

When I answered the call to lead this particular flock I began to see them as the ingredients needed to make a new taste in a community that would be loved and needed. These people, who had been one part, bitter, twice turned away, those who had been dashed with disappointment, dry as flour when it came to love, and as slippery and sly as vegetable oil that had been spilled over the floor. Those who were quick to say they love you to your face and in the next minute be the same ones to persecute your wife and children left a bad taste in my mouth in the name of ministry. It had an oxymoronic nature that perplexed me, yet it filled my heart with joy to know that I was answering the call of God. I had no choice on who could stay and who could leave because they were already there. I could only use what I was given or destroy it by not being a good shepherd.

Because of their hurt they did everything possible to discourage me. They stood in front of the church or at their cars at the end of each church session, including Bible study until I came out of the building to let me know they were watching and talking about me. They would sit in the presence of the word of the living God as it was being preached and not give reverence or praise because of their hate for me. They would do so much over the course of time that it made me want to act counter to the word and will of God. I know it's cliché but I am but a man who has limits. Thank God that He never allowed me to show that I was but a man. God covered me and I had to show the supernatural anointing that was on my life and the life that was in the ministry I was called to lead.

ANONYMITY RAISED A NEW COMMUNITY

One of the most glaring and vivid things I remember is going out of town with my wife and children and upon our return home we had a letter addressed to us from the church in our mailbox. I immediately remembering feeling uncomfortable about the letter but I trusted God that whatever was contained in the letter He would use to show my innocence. He did but later. As you read portions this letter take for a moment to go into my emotions. Imagine the pain I felt when these people openly attacked me at my home, where my family lived. Who I had worked so hard to protect, just thinking about it stirs uncomfortable emotions in me to this day, but that's what happened to us. We think we are over something we prayed about and we do our best to move forward but Satan is so tricky that he will make every effort to call back into memory the one thing that was designed to kill us and take us away from our calling.

This anonymous letter was designed to attack me and the chairman of the deacons' integrity but it turned out to work in our favor. It led a new charge from members who were becoming fed up with the attacks. The enemy had the audacity to mail the letter to people they believed had power enough to corner me. But it worked in our favor. It was designed to cause doubt and speculation towards my decision making but it worked in our favor. Its intention was to get me to admit to manipulation and deceit that was conjured up in their minds but it worked in our favor! As you read keep in mind what Romans 8:28 say, *"and we know all things work together for good for those who love The Lord and are called according to his purpose."*

Greetings NFBC Member,

This newsletter is to enlighten you on some business of the church that cannot be addressed by church members, Deacons &

Trustees without being an outcast by the Pastor. We believe that every church member has a right to know what is going on inside your church. Honestly, if you don't stand for something, you will fall for anything. It's time for people to know what is going on and it's time to stand for what is right. Instead the church body is being told that we are attacking the Pastor ... but who's saying this? None other than the Pastor himself. That's the only way he can get the focus off of all the wrongdoings that he's guilty of. This newsletter is to enlighten the church members of things that are hidden under the cover and not allowed to be questioned or addressed at a business meeting.

Ask yourself ... Can the pastor do as he likes?

The answer is always to be found within a church's By-Laws. Where are your church's by-laws or rules (something else conjured up by the Pastor)? If you had them you would know that the information contained in them have been changed and formatted to fit what the Pastor wants you to believe is true. But if you pull any church by-laws from the internet or just read your bible you would know what it says about being a Pastor or a Deacon. What we have here is just friends, homeboys and yes men. However a wise Pastor, realizing he does not possess all wisdom, will surround himself with spiritually mature men and women of wisdom; integrity; leading righteous lifestyles;

excellence in their personal lives' understanding of financial principles; and having a "good report" within the congregation and the community. He should not be looking for "Yes Men," but men and women who will contend for what are right, according to scripture and the law of the land. With this being said ... let's discuss facts:

Fact #1 ... Our former Chairman of the Deacon Board is an Ordained Deacon, a seasoned saint, a dedicated Christian that was appointed by the church body when the church was formed was sat down and relieved of his duties as the chairman.

Fact # 2....He has also sat ministers down

Lastly and fact # 3 ... Rev. Diggs only wants to be surrounded by young people.

Members of New Fellowship Baptist Church, it's up to you and it's your right as a tithing member to know what is going on in your church and that our Pastor is not who he says he is. Clearly, if God were leading we would not be in an unfinished church today, where we cannot feed a bereaved family or a church that does not have a water fountain. Members, let's not quickly forget how we came together for prayer on Saturday's to find a lock on the building at one time. Clearly our Pastor was caught off guard just as we were. We have a Pastor that changes with the wind. If God dwelled in the temple where we worship, there would be more than the Pastor and a few of his friends in leadership positions.

One more thing read the book of 1st Samuel on how God took his hands off Saul and left him to himself. He didn't even know that he didn't know.

We pray this newsletter is enough to bring some awareness to our surroundings and pray that God will open our eyes to what's going on within our church.

Prayed for and Heavily Prayed over,

Concerned for N.F.B.C. **ANONYMOUS**

Obviously this was the work of more than one person being upset that they were sat down or reprimanded under my leadership. This anonymous letter, I believe, was the handy work of the devil and thus they believed that this letter would be the knockout punch to end my leadership. Oh, but on the contrary, let me remind you what the Bible says in Luke 6:22-23, *"Blessed are you when people hate you, when they exclude you and insult you and reject your name as evil, because of the Son of Man. Rejoice in that day and leap for joy, because great is your reward in heaven. For that is how their ancestors treated the prophets."*

I am not going to lie … I didn't want to wait until I got to church on Sunday to deal with this persecution. I wanted to pay a visit to the houses of each of those who I believed had their hands involved with writing this letter but I heard God say it was an opportunity to rejoice. In order to enjoy the blessings that came from my persecution I had to be attacked. This letter validated our ministry. I wanted to know at that moment why I was being attacked so much. Then God whispered to me that faith is a gift that will only be used tremendously by those who are willing to fight to enjoy its effectiveness. I was willing to stand and use my faith at any cost. God told me, "You will have to fight through ridicule and follow the roadway of risks to be recognized as a person of faith!"

AND NOW WE KNOW

Do you remember my love for cake batter? The bitter sting of past hurts, railing accusations, and persecution had to be looked at as ingredients needed for a tasteful ministry. Because of this anonymous letter, (why anonymous if you're bold enough to mail it to so many people), drew a line in the sand between real supporters of the vision and counterfeit followers of the church. Those who did not want to be accused of conspiring in the letter became die hard supporters because they valued what they were being taught at New Fellowship during that season of attacks. Keep in mind, that episode was not just about a pastor being attacked but it was an opportunity to put on display to others who had been attacked on how to handle that kind of demonic behavior. That was the greatest opportunity I had to prove that my faith was genuine.

Do you think you have that kind of faith? The Job kind of faith that allows you to endure loss of possessions, loss of friends and even the loss of your children and loved ones? I can honestly say that most people do not possess that kind of faith. Instead they have the very opposite of the kind of faith that Job had. We, and I will include myself in that, have the kind of faith that oftentimes must be proven, that diminishes, or even vanishes when too many or a significant loss occurs in our life. It's sad to say that we all, even the strongest Christian have lost a little faith … and it usually comes when we are close to our breaking point and God is truly ready to use us and take us to another level.

That breaking can only be for your good when you allow God to do the breaking and you truly submit to the breaking process. The feeling of that moment can affect you for a lifetime! I cried out so many times, 'Lord, please explain your meaning of faith to me.' I wanted to know if I had it, how do I keep it, and how will it make me stronger. I wanted to know why I was setup by the God I was so determined to chase after and serve.

Everyone in Hebrews 11 went through ridicule and shame but they were willing to risk everything just for their faith, just so others could witness that they truly had unshakable faith. There were blessings that came from their rejections. The people in Hebrews 11 were outcasts, underdogs who allowed God to use them in a major way. Many days they were tormented but they were not willing to sacrifice their faith because of it. I was not willing to sacrifice my faith just because I was being tormented. My persecution made me more determined and even more disciplined to be upstanding and upright.

The misconception of this kind of faith for Christians is that they are required to have all the faith in the world. In reality God doesn't have that demand on us. He doesn't demand that you prove your faithfulness; he requires we have faith to prove his graciousness. Having faith in God always leads us to witness the glory of God to others. It was only after Job's ordeal that the glory of God showed up in the final chapters. And the story of Job became my strength and my refuge. I can even call it my breakthrough because Job had an unshakeable faith regardless of the things and people he lost. He only knew one thing during his trial, that he had to remain faithful to God.

The people I was asked to lead had adopted a crippling philosophy. They believed that they had the right to appoint a new leader before he was anointed by God. They truly believed that it was their job, so to speak, to seek out and find the man of God that would lead them to the proverbial Promised Land. How short sighted they were because it should always be the other way around. The leader should be anointed first. They had a problem that I was anointed before they appointed me. They didn't see that I was God's choice before I was ever theirs. Knowing that I was called was the perfect example of trying to tell people about faith. In today's times, why would a person have faith when everything is evidence based? People are desensitized by reality TV, violence, and other nonsense that crowd their ability to hear the call God has placed on their life. This call can only be heard with an ear of faith.

In Ephesians 4:11-13, *"So Christ himself gave the apostles, the prophets, the evangelists, the pastors and teachers, to equip his people for works of service, so that the body of Christ may be built up until we all reach unity in the faith and in the knowledge of the Son of God and become mature, attaining to the whole measure of the fullness of Christ."* My accusers refused to accept Christ for who He was in my life and theirs. They constantly sought after the agenda that they thought I had. They wanted to see me fall from the grace of God like a castaway. They didn't care about the instructions God had given me. They only cared that their hearts were set on my destruction. Remember, I told you that they were previously hurt by the man of God that they trusted. So I was just a pawn in their plot to destroy any man of God. I am convinced that they only wanted a good preacher and not a pastor to lead them.

And anyone who has been faced with the assignment of building a structure, be it from the word of God or from other sources, they must first have a solid and trusty foundation. Foundations are critical when it comes to building. Whether you are building a building that is massive or small, the foundation will always let it be known if what you are building was built to last. The Empire State Building, as tall as it is, is still one of the most secure structures. Even after severe weather conditions over the years, it is still standing. It has even endured some face lifts, if you will, yet, its foundation is still intact. Why? Because as high as it went its foundation is buried deep in the ground and not on the concrete that many New Yorkers walk on. If it were only supported by the concrete then it would have fallen over at the first strong storm and many would have perished. Having God as your foundation will always give you enough weather any storm and to start all over again if you have to.

It amazes me how so many pastors want to build mega churches without the foundational laying they need first-that being the word of God and the word from God to build. He told me to build and I fought it … but in case you didn't know how God works, He has a way to get out of you what He put in you. In my case, the building of a church was one of my assignments in this ministry. Here is how things went down when I got the assignment:

- June 2008. We had 70 members, $75,000 in the bank and a million dollar vision to build a church on land that we didn't have. I had to constantly answer was it real, or was it all just a dream.
- August 2008: I stood in the pulpit and told the church that we were going to build a million dollar facility on land we did not have. Mind you I had been looking for building for us across the city and couldn't find anything.
- September 2008: Chairman of Trustees came to me and told me about property for sale. The cost was $250,000 and we only had $200,000 in the bank.
- September 2008: We fasted for one month to seek an answer from God.
- October 2008: The property was reduced to $150,000. This caused concern for me and when I went to investigate I was told that there was a dead gas line at the

top of the property and no one wanted to pay the additional $50,000 to have it removed.

- October 2008: I went to the church and told them we will fast for direction regarding the property.
- November 2008: the price of the land dropped 80,000 and God told me to buy the property.
- November 2008: We paid cash for the property and that was enough for the bank to see that we were serious with building our facility.

To this day I believe that faith is not faith if you got to see it before you believe it! There must be a period of improbability before God performs the impossible. I didn't have anything to see during this process. All I heard was God telling me what to do. And in my desires to please and be pleasing to God I did everything that He told me to do without fail or hesitation. I was determined to prove myself to be a righteous man of God and an even more righteous pastor.

Have you ever felt pain for doing what was right? I felt this pain every day of my life for the three years I had to endure the building process. It was painful to look at my wife who wanted to help but we both knew she couldn't, not like I needed. It was painful to stand in the pulpit and preach a word of encouragement when I was the most discouraged man on the planet. It was hard to not yell at my accusers or lose my temper. I knew that for so many years, I was held captive to my temper because I made a habit out of fighting people to prove my worth. I couldn't fight because I was told to build and in building I was not only building a building I was tearing down my limitations.

Philippians 3:12-19 says, *"Not that I have already obtained all this, or have already arrived at my goal, but I press on to take hold of that for which Christ Jesus took hold of me. Brothers and sisters, I do not consider myself yet to have taken hold of it. But one thing I do: Forgetting what is behind and straining toward what is ahead, I press on toward the goal to win the prize for which God has called me heavenward in Christ Jesus. Their destiny is destruction, their god is their stomach, and their glory is in their shame. Their mind is set on earthly things."* I continually had to press on to do exactly what God told me to do… build.

I want you to imagine, for a minute, what it feels like to receive an assignment to help release a unique group of people. You examine them and the situation with extreme caution and secure a complete understanding of your assignment. You execute the assignment to the best of your ability only to discover that the people you were assigned to protect reject your efforts. They reject you because they themselves were on assignment to assassinate your character but yet God instilled in you the faith to build you into the warrior He needs and who was truly after His heart. Do you realize the strength, courage, and faith that must take? If you don't, then read this passage 2 Cor. 4:16-18: *"Therefore we do not lose heart. Though outwardly we are wasting away, yet inwardly we are being renewed day by day. For our light and momentary troubles are achieving for us an eternal glory that far outweighs them all. So we fix our eyes not on what is seen, but on what is unseen, since what is seen is temporary, but what is unseen is eternal."*

I knew that for them the feeling of freedom was so foreign that they refused or just couldn't even recognize a way out of their bondage even with it standing in front of them delivering the message of salvation every week. The hurt I experienced came because I know why I was there but they didn't. So the one thing that kept me motivated to continue is the idea of presenting to the prisoners what freedom looked like according to the will and word of God. I had to realize that I was there not for the building of a structure but also for the building of a people.

It is the following of God that can lead you to some strange people, places, and things. Jesus said, *'blessed are they that are persecuted for my name sake.'* And I was constantly persecuted because I was willing to step out on the only thing I truly had, my faith, to build a church with no history in ministry or shepherding. So if you are having a trial in the midst of where you are sent to teach and spiritually free captured people, then I want to be the first to say, "Welcome to the ministry of following righteousness."

I have to ask you this, have you ever felt wrong for doing what was right? Oftentimes, it's religious folks who make you feel wrong for doing right. That's amazing. While we are all sinful creatures it's the people with no desire to truly have a relationship with Christ who can make even your praise a bad experience. They sit every Sunday in the same seat. They refuse to lift their hands or join the congregation in praise in worship. They only testify from a judgmental viewpoint. You know that viewpoint that says 'Sister So and So' or 'Brother Over There' is doing this. They are spotless in their eyes but are the most polluted people in the eyes of God. You pray for these people and they openly believe that your motive for praying for them is to kill them. The nerve, I know but its true… oftentimes religious folks are the worse.

I recall several sermons where I openly prayed for those who openly sought to destroy me. I stood in that pulpit or rather at the podium in front of my jurors and pleaded my case that I was a righteous man and that God gave me the orders to march forward with building the church. My convictions were so strong to where I told them from the pulpit that if they believed I was using the congregation and my position for selfish gain to pray to God that he would show them who Patrick J. Diggs really was. I knew I would be persecuted so I openly prayed for my accusers. I didn't realize that every open prayer for healing was another docket that was being used against me. They were compiling evidence against my character because they recalled how their last leader openly criticized and shamed them. I was doing neither. I was making an attempt to pray for them and to work towards unity rather than division.

> *"All this is evidence that God's judgment is right, and as a result you will be counted worthy of the kingdom of God, for which you are suffering. God is just: He will pay back trouble to those who trouble you and give relief to*

you who are troubled, and to us as well. ... He will punish those who do not know God and do not obey the gospel of our Lord Jesus. They will be punished with everlasting destruction and shut out from the presence of the Lord and from the glory of his might on the day he comes to be glorified in his holy people and to be marveled at among all those who have believed. This includes you, because you believed our testimony to you."
(2 Thess. 1:5-10)

But the race is not given to the swift or the mighty but to those who are willing to endure to the end. I was in a fight for my faith and I was not willing to walk away with showing God that I was willing to perish to protect His vision and His trust in me. I encourage you that you have to be that ride or die believer in Christ. Knowing that when all things come against you that God is there for you, protecting you and ready to fight on your behalf. Matter of fact, take a moment to read the Book of Esther. Haman was determined to kill Mordecai that he put out a decree that was going to not only going to kill Mordecai, but all the Jews in the land of Xerxes including Queen Esther.

Haman was blinded by his fury that Mordecai refused to bow to him that he convinced the king of the Jews wrongdoing. But God had a plan to not only use Esther but Mordecai because he let Mordecai save the king's life against an assassination plot and used Esther to protect her people, even at the risk of being killed herself. The outcome, the 75 foot gallows that Haman built for Mordecai was used for him and his sons. God never sleeps on your behalf, especially when you are willing to give it all up to serve him. Who are you, Haman, Mordecai or Esther when it comes to carrying out an assignment? They all had an assignment, but only one ended up losing because of his motives.

FAITH FACT

If you are expecting something to happen that will be for your benefit, you give substance (ingredients) to it, then it is no longer a thought but something tangible.

1. What are some of the ingredients that you need to have stronger faith?
2. What do you believe are some of the substances you need to have a better journey?
3. Discuss the oxymoronic nature of your faith. That's having faith when it looks impossible.

CHAPTER 4

A MOMENTARY BREAKDOWN

"When people have a dispute, they are to take it to court and the judges will decide the case, acquitting the innocent and condemning the guilty. If the guilty person deserves to be beaten, the judge shall make them lie down and have them flogged in his presence with the number of lashes the crime deserves, but the judge must not impose more than forty lashes."
Deuteronomy 25:1-3

When other pastors and some members heard that we were building a new church and that we were only three years old we began to be ridiculed for believing that God told us to build. I am reminded when Sanballat ridiculed the Jews for rebuilding the wall. He uttered out in Nehemiah, "What are those feeble Jews doing? Will they restore their wall? Will they offer sacrifices? Will they finish in a day? Can they bring the stones back to life from those heaps of rubble-burned as they are?

> *"When all our enemies heard about this, all the surrounding nations were afraid and lost their self-confidence, because they realized that this work had been done with the help of our God."* Nehemiah 6:16

No, we were not asked those same questions. We were asked, "What are you doing? Don't you know that you won't last in this recession? We encountered so many naysayers who openly opposed the belief that God could do something bigger than any of us ever imagined for someone who was considered an unknown. We were building at a time when the economy had just tanked out and the banks were withholding money from any and every one fearing their own financial ruin. While I had those who opposed me, I was still charged with the task that God had given me in 2008 … 'build my church.' But God said build and I was determined to be obedient to Him because He knew He could trust me.

I was questioned by everyone even the church's self-appointed jury. They questioned every move I made, even the ones I didn't make. At some point, I even started to doubt myself during those times. It was hard looking at myself in the mirror and doubting what God clearly told me to do. I asked myself over and over again, 'Was I doing the right thing?' That's what I constantly asked myself as I started to withdraw from my family, from my wife and my then one year old son. I didn't want to be daddy, husband, Pastor, I just wanted to be done with all of those people and I can honestly say there were times when I wanted to be done with God. I know that's strong to say but if you are truly honest with yourself and trust in the living God with everything in you, then you know that there have been situations, circumstances, and people in your life who have made you want to give up on God or at least the purpose or calling on your life. We all do it but we all don't admit it.

My sister preached a sermon entitled, *All I Have is What God Said.* That became my testimony and by the way, my only evidence. But how can you prove that kind of evidence of hearing God and it not be manifested. I mean we had trouble getting approved for the loan. We had trouble getting the church built in the time it was promised to be built in. We had trouble with every aspect of the project especially from within the church but again, I can't tell you why or what. I can only tell you that God told me to build His church and that's exactly what I was determined to do. But just like Moses, the naysayers started to get to me. Not just my faith but also to my belief in what I heard.

During the building process we started and stopped several times. After more than a year's battle to get the loan we needed we went through complete chaos with getting it built and the general contractor that we hired. But let me back up and tell you about the loan process. When I heard God specifically say, 'build,' I went to the church and they said. 'let's do it.' Of course I didn't know then that answering God would cause the members of the church to persecute me. We worked with Regions Bank loan officer, Mrs. Shannon, who initially said no to our loan but later admitted that something (God) was urging her to help us get the loan. Over the course of the loan process she helped us tremendously, and she would eventually someone I would minister to personally. Shannon was sent from God I have no doubt about that because she too also endured persecution and it wasn't even her battle to fight.

How many times have the no's in your life caused you to take pause and stop what you said God told you to do? How many times have the stress of bills with no money and no one to borrow or get the money from caused you to throw up your hands and shrink away in defeat? We were feeling that same rejection because we had applied to at least seven banks and all of them told us no. We were told what we already knew, that we were not qualified because of our history, not for the amount that we were seeking. But God was working some things out and moving other things for His glory and the strengthening of our faith, especially mine. I believe that, not because I was on the receiving end but because I know the God that I serve is amazing at on-time blessings.

After a year of not speaking to Shannon, she called, and her exact words were, *"I don't know why but I am going to help you get that loan."* She knew our situation and our church history. We didn't qualify but again when God is in the mix and His hand is on you with His favor, you can have no understanding of the assignment before you but He will always make a way. He is definitely a way maker. Shannon started to work with our treasurer to help us get our financial paperwork in order because our previous system was shameful and unmaintained. Even through that she was still gracious and determined to be obedient despite not knowing to what.

She helped us with the hiring of a professional certified public accountant who took our financial records out of the stone ages and into the 21st century of being organized. I received so much persecution from this, as did Shannon. The congregation wanted to know what her connection to the church and to me was. They lightly accused us of being more than business constituents and I admitted that we were. She was sent on assignment by God to help get us that loan and I was sent to minister to her and her husband with cancer and to cover them with the word, something she did not have enough of in her life at that time. My prosecutors even went as far as to call a private meeting with Shannon and me to discuss the so-called shady dealings that they believed were taking place.

Shannon was an angel about that and for three hours she allowed her practices, her integrity, and character to be attacked and on display. She answered ever perverse question they threw at her including the questions I felt were a reflection of ignorance that housed up inside these believers. At the end of the session and after they barked and hissed all the questions they could, Shannon told me she clearly saw my struggle to bring dignity and righteousness to our ministry. She commended me and went on about her assignment of securing the loan for us. Shannon's dedication to us eventually cost her her job at the bank but it did a great work on faith. The loss of that job freed her from bondages that she carried every day of her life in the workplace and didn't realize.

Are you carrying burdens? If you are, then it's time that you let it go so God can use you. God can't use what's not willing to release to allow Him inside. God cannot and will not dwell with negativity or fear. The two cannot coexist. Shannon was able to release so much during the time that she managed our loan and I learned a lot about the people around me as well as about myself. Releasing is necessary in any ministry that you ask God to bless you with. Matter of fact, it's necessary just to walk in a purpose driven life.

"The Lord knows how to rescue godly men from trials." 2 Peter 2:9 NIV

I had to remember that the building of the building was far greater than I could imagine and others could see. For them it was an ego thing because I was a new pastor. But for me, it was about sticking with Christ as He had continuously stuck with me and being obedient to His will for my life, even if I didn't like it.

For Shannon, I assume, it was about breaking some of the strongholds that kept her in pain emotionally and physically.

THE HUMILITY OF BEING BUILT

Before I go into some of the details of building our new church, I had to be broken and lose the one thing I clung to, my pride. Remember I was always the underdog and I always felt that I had to prove myself. I worked tirelessly to show people that I was better than even when God said I had already won. I had to learn humility to the letter and I don't regret not one moment of the breaking that God put me through. I read a book entitled, *Leadership Secrets from the Bible* by Lorin Woolfe and in this wonderful book about being a leader Woolfe shares a quote from Steven Covey, educator, author and businessman:

Humility says, "I am not in control; principles ultimately govern and control." That takes humility because the traditional mind-set is "I am in control" … This mind-set leads to arrogance- the sort of pride that comes before the fall. [One is reminded of characters like King Saul, Samson and Haman here.] But Jesus took break, blessed it, broke it, and gave it to the people. The reason I survived my breaking season while being built was because, like the bread, Jesus blessed me before He broke me. You have to understand the blessing in being broken during your trials and tribulations. Don't worry you will survive because in that season you have been blessed by Jesus Christ.

When we finally got approved for the loan we had a wonderful praise and worship meeting because it was finally time to build. We had fought our Goliath and won, or so we thought. I didn't know that some of the members of the church were about to send me an even bigger and worse Goliath than the hoops we had to jump through to get the loan. Our new Goliath was our general contractor. A man who had boasted of being a part or lead on several church building projects. This man was a smooth talker and assured me that his experience was credible and worthy of being awarded the contract. I will admit that in my eagerness to move past what the bank had us endure overshadowed my judgment. So I agreed to this man without fully performing the due diligence needed to make sure he was who he said was. I listened and trusted those around me more than I listened to God, who mysteriously got quiet when that season of tribulations started.

Again, our contractor was a charismatic man. He knew what to say and how to win the hearts and sympathy of anyone who was willing to listen and pay attention. I was caught on his words and the desires to deliver what God had showed me. That was where I was caught off guard because I began to have tunnel vision during the assignment that God had placed me. Because of that I failed to see the snares the enemy had laid before me.

Don't we do that though? Don't we get so caught up in wanting to do right that we fail to see the warning signs, the caution tape, and the danger signals when it comes to dealing with a person or thing? We believe we trust God so much that we shut off our discernment and our intuition. But in actuality we are not fully trusting God because somewhere in our tunnel vision to get it done, arrogance creeps in, fear of failing slips in, the what ifs hang around even after we rebuke it and that leads to poor decision making. We allow our supernatural to be tainted by our natural and we leave a slight crack in the door or window and that's how the enemy penetrates. Don't think for one minute that you are free from those kinds of attacks. We all, even the most devout Christian, can allow the enemy to enter into our thoughts or into our lives. We trust God so much that we fail to hear the warnings that He gives us because we think He is going to do everything for us, all we have to do is believe.

> *You foolish person, do you want evidence that faith without deeds is useless? Was not our father Abraham considered righteous for what he did when he offered his son Isaac on the altar? You see that his faith and his actions were working together, and his faith was made complete by what he did. And the scripture was fulfilled that says, "Abraham believed God, and it was credited to him as righteousness," and he was called God's friend. You see that a person is considered righteous by what they do and not by faith alone.* (James 2:20-24, NIV)

Everything started great with the project. We had the blueprints; we had a plan and God's vision; we were ready to start. It was time to build and that's exactly what happened and within a short amount of time we had the framing of our new church up. Then something happened. Well should I say nothing happened and we were at a complete standstill. I immediately contacted our contractor who said that the bank refused to release any funds because something was wrong with the loan. I knew nothing was wrong with the loan because we did everything to the letter. I felt completely ashamed that I was following the will of God because here was a building with nothing but the frame. I felt like Nehemiah… I was there to inspect it but there was nothing to inspect.

This was the first of several times where we would get started and then had to stop abruptly because of a contractor who was less than reputable and definitely on an assignment by Satan to destroy the church God had chosen to build and I had agreed to lead. What we eventually found out about all of the building project delays was that our contractor was stealing money directly from the bank loan. I was not watching what he was taking out of the draw. I trusted that he was doing exactly what he said he was going to do when he said he needed the money for materials. While I had access to the money I left the handling of the loan and church finances to our then treasurer, one of our biggest nemeses, who mind you is working to expose the pastor. She was determined to see my demise publicly even though she was the church's financial gatekeeper and she knew I was not signing any documents, let alone draws for the contractor.

He was so bold that he was getting advances from the money to build the building for the purchase of equipment including our HVAC systems to use for other projects he was on. After months of investigations from the bank, from the board, members, and even from myself, it was determined that the contractor had scammed multiple churches and caused financial liens on several projects throughout the metropolitan areas. This man was notorious for using his charm to gain access to the church's building funds and to use the money for purchases for other projects he was over. We also didn't know that his business partner, at that time, was serving federal time for fraud and money laundering, something his family – our members – failed to divulge but they were adamant in leading the persecution against me.

It was sickening passing by the lot that we purchased and placed a sign up saying 'Future home of New Fellowship Church of Fort Worth, Pastor Patrick J. Diggs.' I was humiliated and ashamed and soon I began slipping into a state of depression. These are the times where the Lord truly began to work on me, in my ditch and trenches during the stopping and starting of this building process. While I was so frustrated with the circumstances, falling for the temptation to become bitter towards the people I was to preach to, I discovered God was changing me from a preacher of the people to a new type of person. He was teaching me all these things happened to me because I was being conditioned to change the culture I had grown too accustomed to.

> *Therefore, I urge you, brothers and sisters, in view of God's mercy, to offer your bodies as a living sacrifice, holy and pleasing to God—this is your true and proper worship. Do not conform to the pattern of this world, but be transformed by the renewing of your mind. Then you*

will be able to test and approve what God's will is—his good, pleasing and perfect will. For by the grace given me I say to every one of you: Do not think of yourself more highly than you ought, but rather think of yourself with sober judgment, in accordance with the faith God has distributed to each of you. (Romans 12:1-3, NIV)

I was comfortable and the people I was chosen and elected to lead could see it. I wanted to be transparent and open with everyone and to everything. I was trying to be my own definition of a renewed creature in Christ. But my attempts to show my changes on my own were failing and it left me opened to be attacked and the attacks against my wife and children. I'd been chosen by God to change what we knew the church to be … tradition and rules. Despite being raised in a traditional Baptist church, I was not a traditional Baptist pastor. I was who God called, trusted, and broke for His greater good. I was being melted down. During this long process I often visited the lowlands of discouragement and my motivation to lead and pastor waned. My desires became a distant memory and every day I had to get up, drive past that lot with a framed building it became more distant every day. The responsibilities of pastoring and leading God's flock were no longer exciting to me and soon I was in a state of full depression.

Don't be alarmed that a man of God is saying that he has battled with depression. You may deal with it daily but don't realize that the things you once enjoyed no longer brings you joy. And no I am not talking about illegal things or worldly things, I am talking about the lack of desire to fellowship with God, to be intimate with God, and to let God love on you through His Word. I lost that desire during this process because I felt as if God had truly abandoned me and that I had been set up to be made a fool of. I even believed that my past sins were not forgiven and that God was using me publicly to show the harvest of past seeds sown were harvesting. If you take time to think about that you will see just how far the enemy can creep into your mind and change all your praise, beliefs, and hopes into doubts, fears, and negativity.

I shut my wife out completely but because she knew that God called us to be together, she stayed steadfast in her prayers for me while I made every attempt to keep her shielded from the truth of what I was going through internally. To give you a little background on my wife, she is the daughter of a pastor so she grew up knowing what to expect from a husband who led ministry. She vowed not be a victim of an overzealous pastor who took on too much at one time and I knew this. But when we began building she would become my first victim of neglect. Because I was sad all the time and felt empty, hopeless and guilty of every sin that I had committed in my life, I shut her out. I would come home and go straight in my bedroom or to my office and sit in the dark. She made every effort to comfort me, to be there for me but I was not in a receiving mode. I just wanted everyone to go away and I even had momentary thoughts of leaving this world to end my suffering.

I am not trying to get you to feel sorry for me but I want you to know that depression is real. It's something that affects us all. There were so many days when I felt pressed down and against the wall. I knew I had to be still and to stand the test but I didn't have the strength. I had difficulty concentrating and I lacked the desire to make even simple decisions like if I wanted to get something to eat with my wife or entertain my son. I literally lost my appetite and I spent a lot of time isolated, sleeping, and hoping that I would never wake up again.

Know that when a Christian deals with depression it seem as if they turned against God. As if we no longer believe in God's goodness and how His mercies avail. I am here to tell you to stop believing that right now because depression or sadness is something we all experience in life. There were great people in the Bible who experienced depression. Yes. The very men who were called out to lead experienced moments of depression and felt as if they wanted to give up and die. The pressure of being chosen was sometimes too unbearable and they wanted to be at peace through their death.

David recorded his bouts with depression in Psalms when he was constantly down trodden and persecuted for being obedient to the will of the Lord. Psalms 42:2 shows how David longed to be with God and not because he was excited about the battles he had won but because he was tired of being persecuted for believing in the word of the living God. I felt just like David when he said in Psalms 42:2, "*My tears have been my food day and night, while people say to me all day long, 'Where is your*

God?'" I felt so close to the trials of David as he uttered in Psalms 42:4, *"These things I remember as I pour out my soul: how I used to go to the house of God under the protection of the Mighty One with shouts of joy and praise among the festive throng."* He went on to say, *'Why, my soul, are you downcast? Why so disturbed within me? Put your hope in God, for I will yet praise him, my Savior and my God. My soul is downcast within me ... I say to God my Rock, 'Why have you forgotten me? Why must I go about mourning, oppressed by the enemy?' My bones suffer mortal agony as my foes taunt me, saying to me all day long, "Where is your God?" Why, my soul, are you downcast? Why so disturbed within me?"*

Depression is real. I didn't eat, sleep, and enjoy the things that I once enjoyed. I just cried and doubted the words that I knew to be true. If you find yourself crying more than normal, not sleeping and staying away from the things that you love, find help.

HOW TO DEAL WITH DEPRESSION AS A CHRISTIAN

When you are dealing with depression, know that you can't do it alone. You have to talk to someone you can trust or even a medical professional. Yes, you have the scripture and you may even have your church but Satan wants to isolate you and then take you out, meaning kill you. I isolated myself and that's when the momentary thoughts of suicide crept in. Those thoughts didn't dwell long because God had and continues to have bigger plans for me. But looking back I realized that I beat depression by doing the following:

Let it out. I had gotten accustomed to holding in my emotions and letting them control my decision-making and my responses as a young man. So when I began to deal with my depression from building the church I knew I couldn't respond how I was used to responding. I had to allow God to change and break me during my season of depression. I had to learn to let it go instead of allowing it to destroy me internally and to destroy those around me externally. I went to McKinney Church for prayer and I told God how I really felt. I mean I held no punches and I uttered to God my frustration, my hatred, my distain, and my hurt. I wanted Him to know how I was really feeling because I felt I couldn't share my true feelings with no one, not even my wife.

Job was so confident of the righteousness of his life that he asked God to give him a public hearing (Job 13:3). But I would speak to the Almighty and desire to argue my case with God. I felt like Job and wanted my righteousness to be publicly placed on trial and I used the pulpit to talk to those who had boldly come against me. I wanted them to know that I was only following the instructions of God to build and I made it a point to point out those who had no evidence against me but sat in the sanctuary every week bearing false witness against my character as a man of God. Some may feel that it was wrong to use the pulpit to air my grievances but I felt so condemned and was deep in my depression that I felt the only thing I could do was plea my innocence before I died. I felt that I had to show them that I was but an instrument in God's holy plan. Like Job requested a public trial, I often requested anyone from the church to come to me at any time to see the church records, to talk to whomever was over the money from the bank … whatever they needed I was willing to provide just to prove my innocence.

Get connected. As I stated before Satan wants to isolate you during your depression because he wants to ensure you never recover. He wants you to be so disconnected from others and from God because he wants to end whatever assignment God has you own. Don't allow yourself to be sifted. Jesus told Peter in Luke 22:31 *Simon, Simon, behold, Satan hath desired to have you, that he may sift you as wheat* … If Peter can be targeted and he was who God built the church on, then you and I are not even a challenge but that doesn't mean that we don't have purpose to complete God's assignment.

During my depression, I was lonely and I disconnected myself from those who could have helped me through this. I told you I even isolated from the one person I know who was called into my life, my wife. But she knew to pray for me. I realized that my family was the most important weapon I had to fight my depression. Satan wanted to keep me isolated so it would end my marriage and damage my children. Isolation is a faith killer. I needed people who could help me and so do you. When you're alone it is easy to think that you are the only one standing for God. But you're not. In the Old Testament Elijah was fleeing from his life in I Kings 19 from Jezebel when God sent an angel to Elijah with food and water. Though he parted ways with his servant, he was not alone because God kept him with company. You have to keep your company and stay connected because it keeps you aware of the fight that we as Christians have to endure when we stand bold on God's promises.

Give thanks. This may be one of the hardest things for a Christian dealing with depression to do because it's hard to praise and worship when you feel the world is crumbling around you. There were times when I didn't have a praise left or a thank you to give to God. I couldn't understand why I said yes but He was continually being silent in the midst of my trial. The people who elected me were causing so much havoc around me that that's what consumed me. I only wanted to be free. But then my wife said something to me after I once again preached my pain to those who were persecuting me. I didn't realize that they were winning because they had me preaching my pain instead of preaching the word of God. She told me, after being frustrated with being shut out, that I needed to stop preaching to those who were hurting me and that I needed to preach to those who were hurt and needed a word. Powerful words from my wife and at that moment it reminded me that I needed to praise God and give thanks. In the midst of all this chaos, I still had people to preach to.

What got me through and helped me turn around and get out of my depression was Job 6:24, *"Teach me and I will be silent make me understand how I have gone astray."*

I went astray so many times. Not in my doings or the handling of the church but in my thoughts and my actions on how I handled my adversity. I took it personally because for me it was personal. But it was all God helping me move past myself and what I had made myself out to be. I couldn't allow my disappointment in a hand full of disgruntled churchgoers to distract me from the call and the changes that the call brought. The people had had the most problems. Some of their problems were so steep and deep with traditions that they were brought back alive among this potentially living ministry. I had to realize that they weren't really fighting with me or against me but rather they were fighting to keep their traditions, the same traditions that hurt them in the first place.

Once the light came on for me I learned that it was all a setup to teach me to deal with people who would come against the Kingdom. After all this is what all of this faith stuff was about … being strong enough to endure the trying of our faith. Jesus said, 'You will be persecuted for my namesake,' Matt. 5:11. And I was. I began to learn the word again. I began to praise again and to worship again like I had done. I started to take time with God again to just thank Him even when I didn't want to or felt like I had nothing to thank Him about. When I realized I was never standing alone I regained my self-worth. I was so determined on focusing on my pain that I ignored the people who I was supposed to be pastoring. But God is still gracious.

Despite my momentary breakdown, they learned how to use their faith to fight while they had been watching me. I no longer had to fight so hard. I had an army of people who were now willing to fight on my behalf and the people who were openly attacking me started to dwindle. I had a group of people who were so fed up with church and the arguing to where they were willing to fight for me. They were helping me fight for my faith. Watching them come to my rescue helped me. That was for me to move past my pain. I encourage you to use your bad situations to move past your pain.

FAITH FACT

If you have a great relationship with God, then a great faith will always accompany it.

1. List out what you believe makes a good relationship with people?
2. Take the qualities that you listed and apply them to your relationship with God.

CHAPTER 5

EVIDENCE

"But someone [a]may well say, "You have faith and I have works; show me your faith without the works, and I will show you my faith by my works."
James 2:18 (NASB)

I was never the type of person who allowed things to happen to me. I was always determined to make things happen for myself regardless of the measures that I had to take. I was determined that life would not push me around and force me to take what it was offering. So I pushed back. I pushed back and I never thought about the reaction, fall out or consequences of my pushing. In my world, it was me constantly having to prove myself. It was nothing more than my ego driven desires to prove others wrong that was constantly leading me to prove unnecessary points to people who didn't matter.

Now I was in a position to submit to the authority … to submit to people that utterly wanted to destroy my character, make me act out of conduct, and who wanted to hurt my family and everything I lived and trusted God for. Finally, I had to decide within myself to either let their hate destroy me or to use my preaching as a means to save them and to save the community that we served weekly. Thank God I chose the latter. It would have been a disgrace to who I was and a complete rejection of God for me to achieve while the neighborhood that I grew up in remained in a spiritual incubator and never changes.

I believe that my spiritual gifts are not confined within the four walls of the church. I have worked in numerous groups and grass roots organizations to help those in need, move past their hurts and pains. I believe that is my spiritual gift. I realized that when I was going through my trials of building the church. It was a difficult time for me and my family but it was necessary for God to bring out in me what He needed to. He also had to strengthen me to bear the weight and responsibility of being the under Shepard for His flock. I was faced with something that was bigger than me.

The Red Sea was 1,400 miles long and 220 miles wide. It had a maximum depth of 7,254 feet in the center of it and it is the habitat to over 1,200 different species. But God took the Israelites through the sea to get away from Pharaoh and his army. God is always proving to us that He is bigger than anything we will ever encounter in our lives. For me it was the challenges I endured with the people of the church and the entire building process. Looking back on those days, the lesson God was trying to teach me was to not focus on having faith but the object of my faith. Today it seems we talk about faith all the time and what happens if we only have the faith and believe. If the object of your faith is not who it ought to be, then you will be disappointed and disillusioned. That faith that I am referring to has to be the faith in God, that's the object of who.

When we believe God's word, sometimes we have to do things that seem ridiculous to the world and to people who don't know Christ. I have often heard it said, 'God always leads in a sane, sensible fashion.' Well that depends on who expresses that opinion. In I Corinthians 1:18 it says, *"The wisdom of God is foolishness to the world."* You do not need to expect the world, the unsaved portion of our population, to understand or approve of what you do when you are acting in accordance to the word of God. If you are trying to do something that will seem sensible, logical and acceptable to others, then stop wasting your time. God will lead you in a way that seems ridiculous to the world.

TRUSTING IN AN IMPOSSIBLE SITUATION

Building a church that was only three years old with no previous history was ridiculous to the world and to some of our members. Sometimes we become so comfortable, we don't want to know what else is possible because we only see what we want. We become focused on our desires and want so much so that we eventually drown out God's vision and His voice. There were times when I was so focused on defending myself that I failed to see that I was fussing at those who persecuted me and ignoring those who needed the word of God. I couldn't move forward, I couldn't pray it away; I couldn't turn back even though I wanted to so many days. Like the Israelites I was facing the Red Sea of impossibility but God is an impossible God of infinite possibilities. Just think about it, if they had turned around and refused to move forward, I believe that they would have had no story to tell about their experience with God. They needed that trial of escape to be a testimony for others who were moving across the impossible.

Believe it or not the impossibility of building a church for a ministry that had no history was nothing more than a test by God to show me to remain faithful and for them to let go of the past hurts. They didn't realize that their past was causing an eclipse to the glory of God. While I was called to lead them as their pastor, the members were constantly looking back into their past from their old pastor. They had been enslaved in their minds, their spirits, and even how they viewed ministry as a whole. They had been mistreated for so long that they didn't even recognize a change was being made for their benefit. But I was determined to live the life of Christ and follow His rule because I didn't want to impede my blessings.

Going forward is not always a good idea. A lot of people went forward with a plan or idea but they ended up going in the wrong direction. You may have followed someone or even led someone down the wrong path. That's when you know that that particular move was not from God and it caused you to forfeit the power of God. Here's the scenario we had during the building process of the church.

I was instructed by God to build the church. I went to my wife, and though she knew it was never the desire for us to build a church but to pastor one as an inheritance, she agreed to support me. I stood in front of the church and told them the vision of God and the persecution began. I was ready to move forward with the vision and that's when the delays bombarded the ministry. Keep in mind I had the vision from God and I was ready to move forward but I didn't have the rest of the plan from God. But He does that. Give you a vision, places you on assignment but doesn't give you the rest of the instructions because He wants to see if you are going to first be obedient.

God tested Abraham just to check to see if he was going to be obedient in Genesis 22, *'Some time later God tested Abraham. He said to him, "Abraham!" "Here I am," he replied.*

Then God said, "Take your son, your only son, whom you love—Isaac—and go to the region of Moriah. Sacrifice him there as a burnt offering on a mountain I will show you." Early the next morning Abraham got up and loaded his donkey. He took with him two of his servants and his son Isaac. When he had cut enough wood for the burnt offering, he set out for the place God had told him about. His reward for being obedient was to become the Father of ALL nations.

I'm glad God didn't order me to sacrifice one of my four children but I had to get in the position to be willing to do whatever He said. He knows that I have the heart and desire to serve Him. He knew he could trust me. I was after God's heart and it was my desire to please Him with my obedience. When I got off my face from my prayer and took heed to His command for me to build the church I knew that I would face challenges because of my obedience.

You have to be willing to do whatever it takes to do the will of God. The road will be difficult, there is no doubt about it but if you remain steadfast, the Lord will shield you. When you go forth in the word of God, and you learn how to be still, you are then ready to go forth. You will be able to withstand armies that are great, obstacles that are challenging because the miracle will be greater than it all. God will never allow the obstacles you face to be greater than the miracle. Everything you do as you walk forth in God's will for your life will cause the enemy to challenge you but remember that God is greater than it all. When your enemies are great, your elevation will be greater. When your burdens are great, your blessings will be greater. Going forth means you go in power and God has to honor your faith with His force.

ANSWER THE CALL AND KEEP THE FAITH

One of the greatest truths throughout the word of God is that what we do will reveal to the world who we are. How we live proves who we are or are not in God's sight. God judges us by our works. Will you past the test? Don't get me wrong, you can't work enough to obtain salvation. The true mark of a faith walker cannot be seen in what they profess but by what they produce. Faith can be defined as believing what you don't see and it rewards you with seeing what you believe. Going back to James 2, a person with dead faith cannot produce work that is righteous and rewarding and the absence of work is evident of an absent faith. I saw this week in and week out, the absence of faith of those who elected me to pastor them. They didn't believe that God commanded me to build the church and even though they said they were with me and that I was a man of God, they didn't believe or have the faith needed.

Nicodemus came to Jesus and said, *"I know you come from God because of what you do."* Jesus responded, *"No matter how sincere you are in professing me as God unless you believe and do what I say you are not my disciple."* It's not what you profess but what you produce. They initially professed their desires to follow the ministry but when it came time for them to show their faith that God was using us, then things changed dramatically. They went from believing in the miracles of God to questioning everything I did and the direction of the ministry. What do you do when those closest to you stop believing in the vision? This is a question that I often asked myself because those closest to me in the ministry were the ones who stopped believing in the ministry and its vision.

In James 1:12 it says, *blessed is the one who perseveres under trial because, having stood the test, that person will receive the crown of life that the Lord has promised to those who love him. When tempted, no one should say, "God is tempting me." For God cannot be tempted by evil, nor does he tempt anyone; but each person is tempted when they are dragged away by their own evil desire and enticed. Then, after desire has conceived, it gives birth to sin; and sin, when it is full-grown, gives birth to death.* The faith you exercise to go to God is the same faith you must have to produce for God. I had to have unshakeable faith and believe even when I didn't understand what was going on. I had to exercise my faith and so do you. Just like you exercise your muscles, you have to exercise your faith. Someone once said, "Little faith will get your soul to heaven, but great faith will bring heave to your soul."

A faith that doesn't require a sacrifice really isn't faith at all. It's a pretentious faith that expects something without given up anything in return. If you are unwilling to take a chance with God, you will never discover what walking by faith is all about. If you have to have all the answers before you make a decision and if you're afraid to take a step unless you know things will work out to your advantage, then faith will always be a mystery to you. Life is either a risky ride with God, or an insatiable dissatisfaction caused by a lack of movement in our feet.

You believe that you can pick up the phone and call someone 10 states away but you don't believe in putting $10 in the collection plate. You believe that your job will pay you on every payday but you have difficulty believing that God will make a way in your rough times. Just as sure as you believe in God's miracles for others, you don't really believe in miracles for yourself. It's time to activate your faith and to believe that God is able beyond your understanding.

DISCOURAGEMENT IS SATAN'S WORK

Being discouraged when God is using you is normal. It doesn't stop it from hurting but it is normal because Satan is working to get you off your game. Discouragement is an indication that you are walking by sight, not by faith. Paul said in 2 Cor. 5:70, "We walk by faith, not by sight." That was the source of his stability and strength. When we walk by faith, with our confidence in the Lord and His promises, it is impossible to be discouraged. But when you walk by sight, trying in your senses, your feelings, and your own understanding, you can easily fall prey to all the deceptions of the world, the flesh, and Satan. When you find yourself discouraged you discover where you have been placing your trust. Give it back to the Lord.

The prefix 'dis' negates or reverses the word it is attached to. If you are discouraged, then you will probably become dissatisfied, discombobulated, dysfunctional, disrespectful, and eventually you will become disconnected. A discouraged person takes courage away from others including himself. A discouraged person weakens, deprives of hope, and tears down others rather than strengthening and building up. Your emotional experience in a situation is not determined by the situation. It's determined by you. I determined the level of pain I went through on a day-to-day basis. Initially, I thought I was strong enough to endure the persecution but then it started to discourage me and I became a discourager myself. I discouraged my wife, I discouraged those who came seeking a word because I was preaching my pain and eventually I discouraged myself. I wanted nothing more than to get away from the people God placed around me to minister to and walk out of their dark places. I dictated the countless hours I spent sulking instead of praising. It was all up to me.

Where do you go to get rid of your pain? Do you call your doctor? Do you go to the hospital? Do you tough it out and believe it will all get better with home remedies or prayer? Whatever method you use to get over your pain, you believe in it when it's time to get better. Pain is said to be God's megaphone and my question to that was, "God did you have to speak so loud?" I was in pain mentally, emotionally, and that caused physical pain because of the depression I endured while building the church. Pain can always be felt in different and difficult assignments but the assignment should always be kept in sight especially when being hurt is not an option.

In September 2012, Dallas Cowboys tight end Jason Witten had a ruptured spleen that should have kept him sidelined for the rest of the season. The determination he had to play is worth mentioning even though I'm not a diehard Cowboy fan. It was a game changer for me as I hope it will be for you. He wanted to play the game that he loved so much to where he offered to sign a waiver sheet to absolve the team of any liabilities in case he suffered additional injuries from playing. He was so passionate about giving his team a chance to win that he refused to blame the team if he would have gotten hurt while playing. If you keep in mind your worth to the overall assignment, then you will be able to endure the pain and maybe even forget about it because the pain keeps you more focused on protecting the greatest investment you have ... yourself! I began to understand that this church needed me more than I needed to be free from my pain. It was all up to me, not them, as to how I viewed my pain. Unfortunately, it took me a while to catch on.

MAKE THE CHOICE

You have a choice to be on top of your situation or problems or to let it be on top of you. David was in the midst of the situation, yet he still went from feeling afraid to feeling encouraged. Instead of cowering like his men, David was encouraged because he felt the presence of the Lord and he fellowshipped with the Lord. It was not the external situation that David focused on but the internal choices that made the differences. I love that. This lets me know that my emotional life is not limited to or dependent on what is happening around me.

And the same goes for you. We are not emotionally limited to what is happening around us. We are responsible for change taking place within us. The Bible reiterates this over and over again.

- James 1:2 tells us, "Count it all joy in the midst of test and trials."
- Jesus tells us in John 16:33, "In me you have peace. In the world you will have tribulations tests and trials, but be of good cheer confident, certain, undaunted for I have overcome this world."
- Then again in John 14:27, "Peace I live with you, My peace I give unto you; not as the world gives, give I unto you. Let not your heart be troubled neither let it be afraid."

Again, you have a choice. You determine how you will experience the events of your journey. The events of the journey do not determine the experience for you. So know that whatever we are going through we can choose what and how we will experience it emotionally. I am trying to encourage you, not condemn you. The enemy of our souls lies and tells us, "You don't have a choice, things are too bad." He will try to get you to give up your freedom from the Lord and your ability to choose. Don't fall for it. You get to choose how to respond mentally, emotionally, and behaviorally. Nowhere is it written that when situations are difficult that you must feel depressed. Feeling bad or stressed in difficult times will happen, but it is not one of the

10 commandments. You don't have to feel bad and if you do, you don't have to remain that way.

Initially, I didn't work hard to stay away from depression. I was in denial that I was depressed but my wife made me realize that I was allowing Satan and my accusers to win. You know that's what he wants to do anyway, win against our faith. He seeks whom he can devour. He is definitely on the prowl to devour those who live to do the will of God. Learn to surrender to God and He will make everything easier for you to bear. Like the song says, sometimes you have to encourage yourself. Here are some of the things that I had to do to change my discouragement to encouragement.

1. **Surrender.** In 1 Samuel 30:1-10, David asked the priest to bring him to ephod which was the special priestly device for determining the will of God. David asked the Lord if he should pursue the enemy, and God said, "Yes!" Then David asked if he and his men would recover their loved ones and their possession, and again, God answered, "Yes!" Notice before David made any move, he first determined the will of God concerning the move. You have to consult God in all things that you do. I stayed in prayer with God during the build. My issue was not that I wasn't praying, rather it was that I started to think of my reputation, what others would say about me, and the attacks that would come against my family.

There are no accidents in life. There are only appointments, be they divine or not. The crises hours of our lives never come as a surprise to God because He knows the end from the beginning and He knows for exactly how long you will need His help. So when the crisis invades your life, the first thing you should do is to surrender to the will of God. To fight God's will by complaining and blaming others will cause you to miss the blessing that God has for you in these experiences. David encouraged himself in the Lord by surrendering to the will of God.

2. **Find Strength.** The next thing David did was ask God for the strength to do what is needed to be done. David and his men were tired from battle, and the emotional strain of the crisis had weakened them. But in obedience to God they rode off in pursuit of the enemy. So, where did David and his men get the strength they needed? The answer is simple, God gave it to them. When God tells you to do something, He always gives you the strength to do it and you need to obey. David depended on God's strength, not his own. You and I can never make it through the crisis if we depend on our own strength and power. We have a wonderful promise in Isaiah 40:31 that is so practical, *"They that wait upon the Lord shall renew their strength; they shall mount up with wings as eagles; they shall run and not be weary, they shall walk and not faint."*

3. **Trust.** David trusted God to do the rest. How would David ever find where his enemies were hiding? And if he

did find them, suppose they were stronger than his army? Was there enough time left? Perhaps the enemy had already killed the wives and little children. So many questions and thoughts went through David's mind but then David turned it all over to God and trusted Him to do the work. You have to trust God when you give Him your problems. David took 100 percent responsibility for his encouragement; he took 100 percent responsibility for moving himself from a negative state of mind and emotion to a positive state of mind and emotion. David took 100 percent responsibility for his emotional well-being.

We have to be like David and guard our emotional well-being 100 percent. Satan attacks us when we are not emotionally strong enough to endure the race that God appointed us to. I had to go back to my roots and start back with lying face down praying at McKinney Memorial Bible Church. I was blessed but I allowed my circumstances to dictate my countenance. I vowed right then and there to pray during my commutes to and from work. It was during those times where I would have the most powerful worship experiences during my trials. I was being transformed and renewed and my worship and praise were returning. Something I had placed on the shelf. God taught me how to worship again and that was how I got through those difficult times.

So it's important for you to find your worship and praise time. It's time to get in the habit of praying more, worshipping more and most importantly, it's time to believe more. Your future depends on it as you trust God to run the race that He assigned you to. It will be difficult, undoubtedly, but believing that God has a bigger purpose than you can ever imagine is far more important than getting bogged down with unnecessary emotions. How are you going to release yourself from the emotional boundaries that you may have been placing yourself in?

FAITH FACT

What you believe means little unless it causes you to wake up from the dream and start working on it.

1. What are some of your dreams that you may have put off?
2. That new journey or project, what are your dreams for it?
3. Do you believe that your dreams are worth investing in and living out?

CHAPTER 6

GOD'S MATH

"Subtractiplication: the mysterious way God subtracts by adding, multiples by dividing and adds by subtracting." Patrick Diggs

Sometimes losing a family member, a significant other, a close friend or even something without a heartbeat like a position can cause a person to experience a different range of emotions. Some people shut down, while others do their best to pick up the pieces and move forward. Yet in still, there are those who carry those losses around with them day in and day out to where it ultimately affects who they are as a person and who they are to become in Christ. For some a significant loss can intensify feelings of rejection, anger, fear and other negative emotions that Satan feeds off of. I am talking about loss because it played a major factor as to why I was openly and continuously attacked for being obedient to the work of God.

As a child I experienced a significant loss, the loss of my father who too was a man of the cloth. I was 12 when he passed away after a diabetic stroke. It not only devastated me that the man that I looked up to was no longer around to guide me into manhood but that I had to now bear things on my own. My father was the world to me and before he passed away he told me that we were going to go fishing when his health got better. That day never came but the anger and betrayal of him leaving me surely did. I was tormented by his loss and angry, so angry and confused as to why he would tell me we were going fishing when he knew, or so I thought, that we were not going to go fishing.

My world began to spin out of control and the competitive nature I once had with my friends in the neighborhood became a battle cry and I was at war with anyone who dared to try me. These are the years that I began to seek approval for being a man, because I had lost my father. He was no longer there to usher me into manhood and tell me if what I was doing was right or wrong. So wrong became my moniker. I worshipped my father but he died too young at the age of 42.

To my sisters, mother, and I my father was the closest image we had of God. I know it sounds strange but to us, he could do no wrong. He was perfect. Now I know that he wasn't perfect, no man but Jesus is perfect, but my father was such a great man of God. Others seemingly worshipped him as well. He was a charismatic leader. My father was a great man but I believe that had he been alive today, I would not be the unconventional pastor that I am today. He was extremely traditional and held true to the principals of Baptist religion and rules. He didn't believe in women being allowed in the pulpit, so my sister would have more than likely faced disapproval from him when she answered her call to preach.

Don't get me wrong my father's methods were effective for his time. I believe my father would have faced several obstacles today being a traditional religious leader in a nontraditional world. He may have had issues connecting with people who were worldlier than they are religious and that may have been a turn off for him. His traditional religious rules have no place for the young or inexperienced Christian who just wants to get to know God. For me I believe that God knew that if He was going to raise up a nation in me, then He couldn't do it in the presence of possible competition with my father. Please do not think I am saying that God killed my father so I could get a chance to preach. What I am saying is that sometimes God removes someone from our life so our purpose can be birthed. It sounds crass but when God has a plan to use you then He will move whatever and whomever He needs to.

So God removed what could have been a hindrance to my call, my devout faith to my father. I told you I worshipped my father so I honestly had no room to truly worship God. I know now that God wanted to do great wonders in my life, but He wanted to do a wonder in me first. I had to go through losing my earthly father to understand God's true intentions but it wasn't until I started building the church that I realized that I was harboring some strong hatred towards my father's death and for God.

Let me say this … God does not kill anyone. He doesn't need another rose in His garden. I don't hold the opinion that God is a murderer. But He will need to remove people from your life who are detrimental to His plans for your future. That simply means He gives you warning signs, places you in isolation or just rearranges some things for your benefit and His glory. Trust me when you are being separated from someone you know you love without a shadow of a doubt it's hard to move forward but it's necessary for your destiny. God knows what He is doing; our only job is to trust Him with an unshakeable faith.

God removes people from our presence because human nature will have you following the wrong people to a dead end. The journey of Moses to free his people, the Israelites, is one of the best stories about God removing people from the path of those He is using. Pharaoh's heart was hardened, and he refused to let the children of Israel go. For his refusal God issued a series of plagues on him and Egypt. Eventually it took Pharaoh losing his son in the plague of firstborns being killed for him to get that God was serious about letting the Israelites go. But even in his agreeing to let them go he still fought to go after them after the beckoning of his wife and was killed, along with his army, when the Red Sea opened to let the Israelites cross, closed and swallowed them up.

Did God kill Pharaoh and his army? No, Pharaoh killed himself and his army because he refused to let go of what God constantly warned him to let go of. You would think after so many plagues and the death of his own son that he would have backed down and gave into the will of God and the power He was commanding through Moses. But Pharaoh was stubborn and he allowed his pain, fear, and other negative emotions cloud his judgment and it literally casted him into his death at the Red Sea. God always gives us a warning when it's time to let go of things that are holding us back.

While I was young and didn't realize why my father was taken from me I do know that God will get what He plants inside of those He chooses out. If it's a praise, worship, or to lead His flock, God will do what needs to be done in order to get His purpose for our lives to come forth. I can say, looking back on losing my father so abruptly, caused me bitterness, anger, fear, and rejection. I felt rejected and abandoned by my earthly father because I didn't understand why he left me to figure my life out. I needed him, or so I thought. Like I said before, I needed my father's approval for everything I did, and I got it. Unfortunately, I would have more than likely carried his ways and his standards of approval into my adulthood and into my way of being a pastor. That was never God's plan.

God didn't kill my father but he did remove the aspect of me idolizing and worshipping him over God. Keep in mind also that my father may have ignored some necessary cautions from his doctor, which could have prevented his untimely demise to diabetes. He may have known then what I had to discover during later.

I realize now, as a man, and during my struggles to get our new facility constructed that I had buried a lot of issues and feelings as it related to my father's death. I was angry and that's why I acted out and led the life that I led in my youth. I told you I was a street pharmacist and one of the most hospitable ones on the streets but I was very smart and calculated in my approach. I didn't play and wasn't taken for a joke but I was never about robbing and deceiving people either. I know it sounds like an oxymoron but it's true. Talk about how God looks out for those He chooses and calls. I was being careless and reckless with my life but God thought enough about me to keep me safe.

When God has purpose for your life, be it to preach, minister the gospel, sing praise and worship songs, or whatever He has chosen and called you to do, be prepared for Him to remove some people close to you who might challenge where He is taking you. Like that old saying goes, "Everyone who is with you can't go where you are going." We have to learn how to let go of people or at least learn when we are following a possible dead end situation.

TRAVELING DOWN A DEAD END STREET

As God was leading the Israelites out of Egypt, He had them change their direction from southeast to direct south. They came directly to the Red Sea which seemed like a dead end but it wasn't. The challenge of the Red Sea became a source of a miracle, the ending of oppression, a feeding source, a powerful testimony … so many things for each of the Israelites. God brought them to this dead end because He needed some relationships to be severed permanently. He needed them to completely and totally depend on Him instead of Pharaoh. God needed to bring them to a point where it looked like everything would be lost if they tried to keep going forward without the person they were used to making it with.

Don't we get like that? We ask God to change our direction, to make a way, to show us where He wants us to go but when He presents us the challenges of our own dead ends, our personal Red Sea, we do exactly like the Israelites and we doubt, grumble, and contemplate returning to that dead relationship or situation. As you can see, you nor I were the first ones to complain about our next level blessings. I complained and groaned during the entire building process. I was shocked at myself for how much I truly complained about having been chosen by God to follow His will. But when I was faced with my personal Red Sea I was ready to turn around and walk away without having the trust in God to watch Him open up a blessing. After all, everything possible went wrong during the building process. But nothing was going wrong during God's building process.

Just like Moses and the Israelites, God was preparing me and His flock to crossover from the hardships of our Pharaoh and the dilapidated building we were fellowshipping in to our own sanctuary. Our previous leader and facilities were in no way what God wanted us to have. We just settled because we were used to expecting the worst. We were bred in the church to expect nothing more than hardships and let downs. Some of the members of the church followed the previous pastor to the dead end and were sorely rejected when they received no relief from the betrayal they experienced. What they failed to see is how God was removing them from the previous pastor's hands into my hands, who He said, "I can trust you to listen to me and I can trust you with a blessing." My position as their pastor was at the end of their Red Sea but they refused to believe even after God opened up the blessing of us getting funded for the new building. They saw what they wanted to see.

I learned that sometimes God will take you the long way, even when it looks like the wrong way because he's trying to teach you His ways. We had one of the longest building processes I've ever heard of. It was challenging even at the best of times but God had to take us on this long journey for us to see and trust His ways. He had to build us into a church and not just a group of people who wanted to worship in a place called the church. God had to train us to trust Him even at a dead end, and we had a lot of them. God literally put us through a three year boot camp because I made up my mind to follow Him without question and without fail. I did feel like a failure, more times than I care to count, but I was determined to be everything God said I was and more.

God told Moses to change direction when He was leading the Israelites. He told me to change my thinking and change how I viewed the people who were a hindrance to the move of God. See the similarity? I didn't have millions of people, I only had a select few who were creating roadblocks and discouraging other members but I, like Moses, still had to change something about myself and it was how I saw those who were attacking me. Anytime you choose to be used by God you have to be willing to change how you think, talk, walk, and see others who don't agree with where God is taking you.

God had Moses backtrack. Initially, it seemed as if Moses was confused and they were weak. Pharaoh felt compelled to reclaim his property and thus engaged in a pursuit, but if you look at it closely, it was God's way of completely severing the ties that Pharaoh had with the Israelites. God had us delayed during the building process so many times and I definitely looked like I was in over my head, but God was using those delays as a counterstrike against the enemies who were waiting to attack us. He delayed us because He needed to sever ties with the contractor, with pastors who had gathered to watch me fail, and from those who called themselves members but were only wolves. God knows exactly what He is doing, never doubt that. You may want go back towards a dead situation but it's not for you to be in and completely sever the relationship so that you have no desire to go back towards that dead end.

I've seen this in marriages, relationships, friendships, in ministry, and even in my personal life. God had me looking confused and looking as if I was weak during this building process and true to fashion, Satan was preparing an attack on me that was surely going to destroy me if I had not had the faith and trust in God that I have. God's purpose is always to get the victory. When we look confused and weak, we are in the right place. Sometimes our troubles get worse before they get better because God needs us to have no human way out of our circumstances. We wonder why God doesn't deliver us when we are in need. We wonder why God seems to be pouring it on and allowing us to get the worse of everything. That's what the Israelites thought. They figured they should have stayed put even though they prayed for a way out.

Why do we do that? Why do we doubt God's intentions even after we've prayed for deliverance? It now boggles me as to why I doubted God when I was facing a dead end during the building process. The ironic thing about my doubt was that I knew without a shadow of a doubt that I was called to build that building and that God trusted me. My problem, like many others is that we fail to trust ourselves in those difficult times. It is not enough to just believe in God, you also have to believe in yourself. We become so fearful of the unknown and what we are not used to that we start to doubt our own calling. It's amazing how fear can handicap even the strongest Christian.

I suppose that when we come face-to-face with our fears and knowing that what we were called to do leads us to a dead end, that's when we begin to have to second guess our motives. Yes, regardless of the purity of your heart, there is such a thing as having ulterior motives. Think about it. God called you to preach, to use your gift, to minister to a complete stranger and when it seems that you are facing a dead end because people turn on you, talk about you, steal from you, or just reject what you have to say, you start to doubt if you are truly doing what God called you to do. You start to wonder if you are forcing your way or if God is truly leading you. Is that the normal thing to do? Doubt yourself? Of course it is because Satan is the author of confusion, never forget that truth. Satan's job is to get us to doubt our belief and faith in God. I said it once and I'll continually say it until you understand that Satan means business when it comes to destroying God's chosen and called.

During our breaks from building rather or dead ends, I remembered Deuteronomy 8:2, *"Remember how the Lord your God led you all the way in the wilderness these forty years, to humble and test you in order to know what was in your heart, whether or not you would keep his commands."* God will stop you dead in your tracks just to get you completely on board with His vision for your life. Too many times we refuse to check what's in our hearts and to allow God to touch the darkest parts of our lives. There will always be a time when we need to be inspected by God, especially when we are on assignment.

Now understand that when you begin to move forward with the will of God for your life, trouble is right around the corner waiting. It's a part of your journey when you accept your assignment or calling. You will never experience a life of complete freedom from troubles and trials. I am a pastor, one who was called by God and I had troubles as soon as I accepted the assignment of building a new church. My trials intensified each day I got up and moved forward with finding the land, getting our finances together for the loan, getting the loan, finding the contractor, and so on. Every time we looked like we were moving forward we were thrust backwards and verbally assaulted.

The challenges were so great that one night after we had church, one of our former musicians approached me in the parking lot. He immediately eluded that he had a weapon and he began to demand full payment for his services even though he missed rehearsals several times. It is church policy that we maintain an orderly music ministry, which include being at rehearsals, but he refused to follow the guidelines, so much so that he felt justified when he approached me in the parking lot demanding his money. I could have lost my natural mind and responded in the natural but instead I remained calm because I realized that Satan was afoot and I refused to give into yet another one of his attacks. I explained to the man that he needed to think about the situation and reminded him of our policies and why he was not getting the money. I know I could have yelled for help but I felt that in that moment we both needed to remain calm and I didn't want to see if he really had a weapon so I controlled my temper. He left without incident and I did not file charges.

I shared that story with you, first to let you know that Satan will go to any lengths to get you to back down, and second for you to understand that attacks come from anywhere, any place, and anyone. I was leaving church when he approached me. God rarely allows us to take the easiest or shortest route when He has called us to lead. That's the testimony we have that no other religious practice can give, God can use bad intentions and incidents to bring glory to His name and something for your good. So remember it's all good. Understand that having problems does not mean you don't have God. You just have to understand that with God, whatever it is; God has a way of working it out for your good.

GOD'S REMOVAL PROCESS

Deciding to take a stand for God and getting rid of some of the people who are weighing you down takes a lot of praying, believing, and trusting in God. You have to have supernatural faith to believe that the person that you decided to tie yourself to in friendship or in love is not the person that needs to remain with you as God takes you to His next level for your life. But you know it has to be done in order for God to use you and trust you with the assignments he has for you. Sometimes the very people we have to cut loose are our family members, such as a parent, child, sibling, or the like. They can weigh us down with their needs and wants that we fail to see or hear what God's next steps are for us. Going back to the story of my father, I know he would have caused me to ignore what God wanted from me because for me my father was my god.

I carried around his death with me so long and I was bitter towards God because I thought He killed my father. But again, God doesn't kill anyone. He is not a serial killer but He will permanently destroy bondages and castaway those who knowingly commit sin, such as the town of Sodom and Gomorra, a filthy place where homosexuality was expected and desired by its citizens. God is a fair and just God who can be angered to wrath by those who refuse to keep His covenant. If you are new to Christ and you read that last statement, then it sounds like I just said follow God or die. That's not what I am saying because God gave us all a choice. What I am saying however, is when you step out on your faith and trust God enough to use you for His glory then it is important that you must maintain His covenant. You must walk in faith like Enoch. Trust like David. Believe like Peter because it's all a part of being called.

I'm so glad that God selected me to lead His sheep, His children but I can say without doubt that there were times I wished in secret and out loud in private that He would get rid of those who opposed me. What I didn't realize, at that time, was that those people who were adamant about tearing me down were the people that He was using to build me up. When my wife instructed me to let them loose and to preach to the ones who needed to hear the word of God, I immediately started to look at my situation differently. I no longer had the energy to fight the fight God had already won for me. I didn't realize that He was using my issues for my benefit and His glory because as they fought me and as I refused to fight back, my character was showing. The trust in God I had was showing, even when I felt like it wasn't. It's amazing how God will set you up. He will use your worse storms and trials to show others His mercy. Will you be able to recognize it and give Him praise?

Once I started to give praise for the situation I was in I started to experience my breakthrough and I started to watch those who opposed me remove themselves from the church or were completely removed from the world through death. The contractor who stole our money and equipment was removed from our lives but his indecencies were exposed before us all. God had to remove him from us so we could understand the power of prayer before moving forward. Our grace to not press charges against this man made him see the error of his ways and he came before the church crying asking for prayers. He might have been playing on our sympathy as a church, but that move he did and the mercy the church showed him eventually showed me the power of forgiveness. I didn't want to forgive him. I wanted to remember every pain he caused me and the ministry during the building process. His family was torn and some of them began harboring resentment for me for exposing him for robbing us. Remember, it was a few of his family members who referred him to us and yet there were others who told me that he was a fraud and thief.

God will remove those people who directly affect your walk once you are called. The people who openly and without reverence to the ministry opposed me and the plan of God either left and went to another church, died with hate in their hearts, or were asked to leave by other members of the church. Yes, as I stood for God but refused to fight, my character was being shaped and the number of people who supported God's vision grew daily. The hearts of the ones who were even against me began to change. They asked several of those members to leave the church if they were not willing to get onboard with God's vision. They had my back. I didn't know that I was making an impact that great but God knew it and that's all that mattered. One of the most vocal naysayers was told to leave the church by an elder member who had had enough of her torment. The elder member had reached her capacity for the disrespect of this woman who sat in the pews and refused to praise, to give, or even speak to me. It was amazing when our member shared that story with me. She felt triumphant that she stood her grounds for God and for me.

BITTERNESS WILL DESTROY YOU

While the naysayers were fleeing, the believers and our membership started to grow by leaps and bounds. It still amazes me how during the chaos God still grew our membership and soon people who were coming to watch the talked about chaos were being changed by the word of God. I preached angry sermons but God used those words to still minister to others who were lost, confused, and who had been betrayed by the person they thought the most of. We have all been there, so you are not abnormal or different when you harbor anger and bitterness in your heart. It's almost impossible not to become bitter when you are constantly attacked for trusting God for it all, not just some of it, but everything you are and who you want to be. Your bitterness can cause you to doubt God's purpose for your life.

I was bitter because I lost my father and I didn't want to get close to any man, not even God. But He had to take me through the impossible for me to understand that He was my father, my only father. Yes, I had an earthly father but my heavenly father had to become my everything. I had to break down and get out of my own way to allow God to completely love me. I couldn't hold in my cries when it was me and God because He knew what I was crying about, internally and externally. God gave me an ounce of grace when I attempted to question Him about my assignment that I signed up for. God held me, rocked me to sleep, and protected me because during those dark days, I welcomed death. God became more to me than you can ever imagine and soon He replaced the absence of my earthly father. God became to me what my father was to me before he passed away. God knew He had to remove my father in order for Him to take His rightful place in my life … being first.

Count it all joy when God removes someone you love from your life, even if it's abrupt because it's always for your good. My father was young but he could have possibly damaged the pastor God was molding me to become. When I finally understood why God took my dad and why He needed to be the most important person in my life, I began to soar. I began to feel alive again and I realized that my "daddy" was not going to let anything happen to me. He was going to test me and allow me to be tempted as well as tested, just like He did with Job and Jesus but He was never going to let Satan take me out.

Take a moment and give God the praises right now. Take the time to openly and loudly proclaim His goodness because that's powerful. God will allow you to be picked on, if you will, but He will not allow Satan to destroy you, once you trust Him with all your heart. God is a just God. We have all had to experience loss of some kind. Loss is always hard to acknowledge and to move past. There is no scripture that says loss is not supposed to hurt. When Jesus was told about Lazarus dying, he wept for His loss even though He knew He had the power to raise him from the dead. Jesus felt the pains of loss. Moses felt the loss of losing his place when he had to flee after he murdered the Egyptian guard, as did his adoptive mother. Loss is inevitable and the pain that comes along with it. But what we can do is make sure the loss doesn't consume us.

I can't give you two steps on how to move past your pain of loss because it took me almost 30 years to let go of being hurt from the death of my father. I had developed thick scar tissue over my heart from that traumatic loss. And going into battle while building the church added to the scars but it also exposed what I was hiding and refused to show. Satan had gotten comfortable inside of my spirit and hidden nuggets of negativity that only God could remove. I am grateful for the experience of the building process because it helped me heal from the loss that I was carrying around.

It's time to let go and to move past those hurts. God wants to use you but He can't as long as you hold onto that thing that Satan meant for your demise. It's time to cry out to God in truth and honesty and tell Him to heal your broken heart. To dry up your well of bitterness and to restore what the devil took away. Don't give another day to your loss. Give praise and know that whatever reason as to why that loss occurred that God is going to give you double for your trouble.

FAITH FACT

Whenever God builds a church of faith, Satan will attempt to build a chapel of doubt close by.

1. List out some of the doubts that you've encountered.
2. Have these doubts caused you to be delayed or denied?
3. How do you believe your faith has allowed you to move past these doubts?

CHAPTER 7

ORDER IN THE CHURCH

*"I will stand on my guard post and station myself on the rampart;
and I will keep watch to see what He will speak to me, and how I
may reply when I am reproved. Then the Lord answered me and
said, "Record the vision and inscribe it on tablets, that the one
who reads it may run. "For the vision is yet for the appointed
time; it hastens toward the goal and it will not fail. Though it
tarries, wait for it; for it will certainly come, it will not delay."*
Habakkuk 2:1-3 (NASB)

Can you remember the last time you were anxiously waiting for something you really wanted? For me, as a child it was Christmas, birthdays, or even summer break. As I got older it became graduation from high school, then from college. For some adults, waiting on something they really wanted might have been their wedding day or divorce, a special award, the birth of a child. For days, weeks, even months you waited until that day finally arrived and with that excitement sometimes you began to worry and became anxious, especially if you experience any challenges during that waiting process. Just think about it … as a child you became anxious if you got in trouble and your gifts were threatened. As a teen or college student it was a failing grade that made you nervous. As an adult it was an argument with your loved one or a possible loss of your job. Challenges cause us to become anxious even when we know we are guaranteed the promise.

That's how we are as Christians. We know we will always get the victory as long as we press towards the will of God but when difficulties arise, we began to doubt and get nervous. It's important to remember that in the Bible it is written that we win! Our journey is never guaranteed to be an easy one but nonetheless we win. Uncertainties lead to doubt and doubt leads to fear which becomes a crippling disease for Christians. Some of you will fall by the wayside and forfeit personal and spiritual progress and gain because you become afraid of what you don't know. That's a reality but it shouldn't be normal for you to give up because things get difficult during your journey.

I was like that. When I heard God tell me to build the church, I immediately became anxious because I had seen other pastors build their churches and even some lose them so I knew I never wanted that to be me. My wife became anxious when I told her what God told me but she supported me anyway. Being anxious never left me and during the building process I became anxious about everything. We got the $1 million loan and the anxiety of making sure every penny was accounted for crept in. I can go on and on about every situation that made me anxious but it's a part of the job when you diligently seek and choose to follow God.

There are still some who will never get around to following God because they don't know the details of why they are following God. They refuse to move forward because they don't know the terms, conditions, who, what, when, where, and how of being obedient and trusting God. That lack of knowledge completely shuts them down and they refuse to move forward. I want to let you in on a little secret … God is not obligated to give us a full page report and concise conclusion of what He wants us to do. When you agree to be used by God the number one thing He wants from you is obedience to His word. That's it. God will even challenge us to do things that seem impossible just to see if we will trust Him, even though He has already trusted us with the assignment.

How many times have you refused to let God use you because you didn't completely understand the reason behind His request? Be honest with yourself because there are no super saints out there. Jonah refused God's request. How many times have you said you can't do something? Think about it. Did you tell God you can't love your enemies? Did you tell God you can't help someone in need because they were not your friends or family? Did you tell God you can't tithe or give an offering because of your finances? Did you tell God that you can't study or learn His word because you didn't have time? Did you tell God you can't be close to that person who hurt you from your past? Now you can see if you are in the 'can't' crowd and how you may have become anxious when God said trust Him.

TRUSTING GOD

When you trust God you may be asked to leave someone you thought you couldn't live without. You may be asked to leave your high paying job for one that pays significantly less. But know that if He is moving you from one place He has plans to increase you in another. The children of Israel, after being in the wilderness for 40 years, learned what it meant to be saved but when it was time for them to move into the Promised Land, they became skeptical. Joshua told them, "You have not passed this way before." But they were still concerned about the great mass of land because some were trying to recall what they saw 40 years ago as children. Yet in still, they trusted Joshua because they loved God and knew what God did for them in those 40 years.

Do you have that same kind of trust? Do you need to be taken through 40 years of hard time just to make sure you are broken down far enough to where God can finally get the praise from you? I hope not. Here are two things that you need to know about the wilderness into the Promised Land situation:

1. Some things you just won't know.
2. You do know that God will be with you.

While we are here, we must expect unusual events to occur and paths that we have never passed before. It's inevitable but if we have the assurance of God's presence, what's the purpose of being fearful? Unfortunately, this is something that we struggle with even with faith.

In order for us to get to where we are going it's important to recognize three distinct categories we experience as we go forward in the purpose of God. The Been Through phase, the Belief phase, and Breakthrough phrase. It's time to help you move past you, to trust the Lord and let go of the pain so God can use you completely. I had to get out of my own way and I want this book to help you.

YOU'VE ALREADY BEEN THROUGH

You can't really accomplish much for God until you have 'been through something' mentally. Let's look at the Israelites, they had all the experience of the 40 years with God in the wilderness. They went through the rough times in the wilderness. They all experienced hunger pains, parched mouths, and uncertainty in the wilderness. But because they had been through their faith was tried, tested and true. Know that you can't say that you really know God until you've been through a wilderness moment and you know He delivered you. Your testimony really doesn't hold a lot of weight until you have been through some wilderness moments. Take a moment to reflect on your wilderness moments. Think about every time you were counted out, God showed up and out and lifted you up. He protected you and guided you through your tough times.

The Israelites only had what they remembered from the past to judge the uncertainty of being able to move into the Promised Land. They only had slave and wilderness experience but the one thing they knew is that despite the future unknowns they had been through something and that gave them a measuring device. For instance, there was the Red Sea before them 40 years ago and now they had the Jordan River. They knew in Joshua 3:15-17 that God took them through the sea and He was now taking them through the river. They went from the known of Egypt to the unknown of the wilderness, now they were being led to move towards the Promised Land, another unknown land. Every day in the wilderness God supplied manna and water for them and they knew He could do it again. They had been through faith and went forward.

You have to know that the reason you can face tomorrow is because you know what God did in your yesterdays. You should never doubt your own experiences with God when He has brought you through. We have to have had 'been through' in order for us to become true believers. God takes us through certain situations to show us He was and is there all the time.

Have you been through too much to turn back? That's why you press forward to go to church. That's why you praise and worship like you do. That's why you have an unshakeable faith in God because you've been through and you know God was with you.

BELIEF IS BELIEVING

The story was told of an atheist who was spending a quiet day fishing when suddenly his boat was attacked by the Loch Ness monster. In one flip, the monster tossed him and his boat high into the air. Then it opened its mouth to swallow them both. As the man sailed head over heels, he cried out, "Oh my God! Help me!" All of a sudden the attack scene froze in place and as the atheist hung in midair a voice came down from the clouds, "I thought you didn't believe in me?" The atheist responded, "Come on God, give me a break. Two minutes ago I didn't believe in the Loch Ness monster either."

I shared that story with you to help you understand that it shouldn't take an extreme situation like this one, although fiction, to get you to believe in God and His word. The earlier generation of Israelites failed to enter into the Promised Land because they were full of unbelief even though they constantly saw the miracles God was performing on their behalf. After 40 years in the wilderness and some of the people dying off, the new generation, led by Joshua and Caleb told the people it was time to move into the promise their ancestors lost out on. Can you imagine how exciting that must have been for the survivors? To finally get a chance to see the promise God made to their ancestors? But with that great excitement there was still doubt and anxiety when they came to the river and fortified city of Jericho.

Challenges in the midst of your excitement are not new. Even with your hopes at its highest, there are challenges and problems that come and if you're not careful you will become doubters of God's word. But something inside of you should cause you to go through your challenges and problems because you believe what's in your heart, that God is with you and able. This is where you really have to ask yourself ... do I really believe in God's word? Ask yourself these questions:

- How do I respond to Philippians 4:13, *"I can do all this through him who gives me strength?"*
- How do I respond to Acts 1:8, *"But you will receive power when the Holy Spirit comes on you; and you will be my witnesses in Jerusalem, and in all Judea and Samaria, and to the ends of the earth."*
- How do I respond to Leviticus 19:18, *"'Do not seek revenge or bear a grudge against anyone among your people, but love your neighbor as yourself. I am the Lord."*

Do you believe that you can trust in God to have faith, love and hope when challenges arise against you? If you believe like you say you do then the words of God should be all encompassing in your life and your accomplishments in the Word should show.

Joshua told the people to consecrate themselves. That simply meant to set aside anything that was unholy if they believed in God. You have to consecrate yourself and get rid of the unholy things that are holding you back. When you do this, you then have the right to expect the unexpected of God. The people of Israel expected God to perform miracles because they prepared themselves. They learned that preparation and dedication results in God's manifestation. If He did it for them, He'll do it for you. He'll show up if you're looking for Him and believing in Him. He'll come through if you act on what He says. God will fix what's broken when you remove the unnecessary stuff you think you must have in your life. It's just that simple ... get ready.

GETTING TO YOUR BREAKTHROUGH

A breakthrough will only happen for those who know how to follow God's lead. He gives specific instructions on how to breakthrough. When it was time for the Israelites to move the soldiers told them in Joshua 3:3-4, *"When you see the ark of the covenant of the Lord your God, and the Levitical priests carrying it, you are to move out from your positions and follow it. Then you will know which way to go, since you have never been this way before. But keep a distance of about two thousand cubits between you and the ark; do not go near it."* This was very important but it's a principle that's often overlooked during our Christian journey. We rush and move before the will of God. How many times have you gotten in a hurry for something that

God wants us to wait on? Don't feel bad, it's inevitable but we have to be sure we stay behind the will of God and wait on Him.

In the bestseller book by Henry Blackaby, *Experiencing God*, he suggested that the best way to live according to God's will is to "watch to see what God is doing, and then join Him." In other words, we must let God take the lead. Some might say, 'we need to wait for an opened door.' Many of the problems of the church are not that we do the wrong things, but that we are doing good things at the wrong time. We moved before God. I admit, I moved fast on getting the contractor because I was excited after getting the loan approved. We were always instructed to build, that's why God made provisions for us, but we might have been able to avoid some of the delays if my eagerness hadn't moved before the will of God.

Timing is everything. In the Christian life, most of the mistakes we make come from us not letting the ark of God go far enough ahead of us before we gather up our belongings and follow it. We run before we are sent, act before we are quite sure that God wills us to do so, and at the root of most of our failures are a lack of patience. It's only getting worse because we have become so attached to instant results. We want everything right now and that has caused some of us to move past God without a second thought. Our haste had become our delay in our building process. A lot of us are impatient and when it comes to uncertainty either in opinion or conduct, we are rushed to make a quick and ill informed decision. We take for granted that God may have delayed us for a specific reason or season. Sometimes

God wants us to wait and watch our surroundings. Then and only then at the appointed time, He will let you know when to move.

Get in the mindset that it's better to wait than to create a self-destructing situation for yourself. That's when we rush and make a mess of things. We either inflict pain on others or cause ourselves to be placed in damaging situations that may utterly destroy our faith. When you move without God you open yourself up for immediate attacks from Satan. Eventually Satan binds you and you lose your power to pray and you can't break away from the snares that he laid for you. That's why it's important for you to wait on God because there are times when you literally have never done something before and God is trying to preserve you.

That doesn't mean turn around and go back. It just means you need to wait on God. In your waiting comes your breakthrough. That's when your real praise will come through. That's when God will open doors you never imagined seeing, let alone opening. God's breakthroughs are twofold, to break you and make you die to yourself and to show His glory. You have to be willing to be broken so God can use you. You'll discover like I did that God uses us best when we're broken for his purposes.

Once you begin the visionary process, you'll discover some things that will discourage you. Doubt, demons, distractions, fear will become your friend because your vision and God's vision will not coincide and go the way you want them to go. Doubt always seems bigger than your dreams but you have to have the faith and perseverance to move forward on

God's time. Separate yourself from people without vision because they are restless, purposeless people who can easily be used by Satan to distract and attack you. I experienced people without vision during the building process. People who were in church every time the doors were opened. They were routine members and when I revealed to them God's vision, God revealed to me their lack of vision. It began to show up and what they thought was their mission to destroy me became an assignment that validated me. I had never been in that situation before. I just knew I was told to do what God said to do.

God eventually isolated me, rather I isolated myself, and in my isolation I realized the things that I had to endure which included persecution, criticism, and doubt. I had to look for the God of process because everything I was going through was a process to deliver me to and through my breakthrough. I had to learn to not respond to the criticism or to the letter that was written to the church and sent to my home. I stood in the pulpit the very next day and said to the congregation, "here is my response, get your phones ready. Let us join together and pray for our enemies." And I stood there in silence and prayed for them and immediately felt free. I didn't expect the outpour of cheers that I received but I wanted the attackers to know that they would not get another day of my time trying to prove my innocence because it was God's battle, not mine.

I had to learn to enjoy the process by understanding God's presence. I began to enjoy a heightened spiritual awareness that brought a divine presence to me and that lead me to receive a promotion in my faith walk. God was pleased with my determination to keep moving forward and soon we went from constant stopping to getting the building completed before the new projected move in date. God sent us a new contractor, lifted the $50,000 in liens that were placed on our property due to our last contractor fraudulent activities and then finally a building that met our needs. The day we worshipped for the first time in our new building was the best promotion I ever received thus far because even in my weakest moments I was steadfast in trusting and believing God. I allowed Him to use the loss of my father, the rejection of so many people, and the backstabbing of the members in the church to break me down so He could pour into me and build me anew.

Remember this if you remember nothing else from this book, at God's appointed time, the vision will be performed. Don't waste time fighting the unnecessary battles of those talking bad about you because you have to conserve your energy for the battles that threaten your purpose. Don't concern yourself with being called names or hearing the opinions of others or being recalled of the rules of religion. The enemy will set you up every time to fight back because at the end of the day all you will have accomplished is being worn down. I defended myself to anyone who listened and it beat me down and had me lying in my bed refusing to face another day. I can't help but thank my wife for sticking it out with me.

Don't get distracted while you are on assignment from God. Maintain the vision God gave you and watch what He reveals in your life. Habakkuk told God after complaining, *"I will stand at my watch and station myself on the ramparts; I will look to see what he will say to me, and what answer I am to give to this complaint."* Despite what He saw Habakkuk was still willing to allow the Lord to pour into him so he could still carry out the vision of God. When the Lord heard his complaints he answered in Habakkuk 2:2, *"Write down the revelation (vision) and make it plain on tablets so that a herald may run with it. For the revelation (vision) awaits an appointed time; it speaks of the end and will not prove false. Though it linger, wait for it; it will certainly come and will not delay."*

See how important it is to wait on God? If Habakkuk teaches you nothing else, it should teach you to see God for a vision until you receive it. Don't try to establish your own vision because in order for it to be successful it has to first originate from God and not from you. God will not fit a man-originated plan into God oriented purpose. When you seek the vision of God, take you out of the vision so you can be completely used by God. *If we seek Him with all our heart, we will find Him and we will know the plan He has for us* (Jeremiah 29:11-13).

It's time to start seeking God. I pray that when you seek Him and He reveals a plan for you that you do like Habakkuk 2:2 'write the vision and make it plain...' then follow God to make sure it's executed correctly.

Faith Fact

You'll never discover the new oceans in your life until you lose sight of your shore.

1. Do you believe that you have lost sight of any part of your dream?
2. How do you believe you will regain it?

ABOUT THE AUTHOR

Patrick J. Diggs is a native of Fort Worth, TX January 10, 1972. He attended schools in Fort Worth Public Schools. He announced his call to preach in 2000 and has been the lead pastor of New Fellowship since 2008 with an active membership of more than 400 members. Diggs life's journey as a pastor would change considerably when he answered God's instructions to build the new facility for New Fellowship on June 1, 2008. Even with very limited funds and membership, God used the faith of a few followers and in November of 2011, along with new members, the doors of New Fellowship opened for its first worship service. Diggs believes in his calling and understands that it takes strong faith as well as a strong church to build strong families.

Diggs works tirelessly and diligently to teach men their God ordained role at home as well as helping them understand the works to get them to become more involved in church to make sure their lives are guided by practical Christian principles. The mission of New Fellowship Church of Fort Worth is to live for Jesus, look for the lost, and love others with the love of Christ.

Diggs is currently enrolled in Southwestern Baptist Theological Seminary and also serves on the JPS Pastoral Council, a Campus Coach for Read2Win, and actively involved the Fort Worth community. Diggs is married to Mary Diggs and has four children Jordan, Britney, Raven, and James Diggs.

ABOUT NEW FELLOWSHIP CHURCH OF FORT WORTH

The vision of New Fellowship Church of Fort Worth is to offer keys to a transformed life through the life of Jesus Christ. We are a non-denominational spirit-filled church with a body of believers who are excited about new life in Jesus Christ. We are free to be who Jesus created us to be!

Our beliefs can be summarized in 1 Corinthians 15:1-4. *"Jesus died for our sins, was buried, was resurrected, and thereby offers salvation to all who will receive Him in faith."* We believe that Christianity is more about a relationship than religious practices. Instead of adhering to a list of "do's and don'ts," the goal of a Christian is to cultivate a close walk with God.

Our mission is to touch and change lives with the love of God and the power of His word. We believe that God has a destiny and purpose for every individual. Therefore, we endeavor to minister God's word in a practical way to help believers grow spiritually, receive God's blessings, and become mighty ambassadors for the Kingdom of God.

Visit us 5420 Flamingo Road, Fort Worth, TX 76119 or call 817-386-5544. We are online at www.newfellowshipchurchfw.org.

www.ingramcontent.com/pod-product-compliance
Lightning Source LLC
Chambersburg PA
CBHW072005040426
42447CB00009B/1495